Sizzling
Second Edition
Summer Reading Programs for
Young Adults

Katharine L. Kan for the
Young Adult Library Services Association

American Library Association
Chicago   2006

Composition by ALA Editions in Sans Extended and Janson Text using QuarkXPress 5.0 on a PC platform

Printed on 50-pound white offset, a pH-neutral stock, and bound in 10-point coated cover stock by McNaughton & Gunn

The paper used in this publication meets the minimum requirements of American National Standard for Information Sciences—Permanence of Paper for Printed Library Materials, ANSI Z39.48-1992. ∞

Library of Congress Cataloging-in-Publication Data

Kan, Katharine.
    Sizzling summer reading programs for young adults / Katharine L. Kan for the Young Adult Library Services Association.— 2nd ed.
        p.   cm.
    Includes bibliographical references and index.
    ISBN 0-8389-3563-X
    1. Young adults' libraries—Activity programs—United States. 2. Teenagers—Books and reading—United States. 3. Reading promotion—United States. I. Young Adult Library Services Association. II. Title.
    Z718.5.K36 2006
    027.62'6—dc22   2005028264

Printed in the United States of America

10   09   08   07   06   5   4   3   2   1

This book is dedicated to all the hardworking young adult librarians and other library staff who work with teens and continually strive to provide the teens in their communities with the best services and programs they can muster.

CONTENTS

INTRODUCTION

In 1998 YALSA (Young Adult Library Services Association) published *Sizzling Summer Reading Programs for Young Adults*, which showcased a number of programs for young adults offered by public libraries across the country. Libraries of all sizes, from small municipal libraries to large metropolitan systems, offered reading programs, special programming, and volunteer opportunities for young adults. So why do we need another book on summer reading programs for teens? In the years since 1998, research has shown that reading skill levels among teens have remained about the same, yet our growing and ever-improving technology demands higher skills. As Stephen Krashen states in *The Power of Reading: Insights from the Research*,

> Nearly everyone in the United States can read and write. They just don't read and write well enough. Although basic literacy has been on the increase for the last century, the demands for literacy have been rising faster. Many people clearly don't read and write well enough to handle the complex literacy demands of modern society.[1]

Patrick Jones and Joel Shoemaker note that nearly one-quarter of library patrons are teens, but less than 15 percent of public libraries have young adult librarians.[2]

READING SCORES RESEARCH

Just how well do American young adults read? The National Assessment of Educational Progress (NAEP) published *The Nation's Report Card: Reading Highlights 2003*, which reported on reading scores of fourth graders and eighth graders.[3] The report compared scores from 1992, 1994, 1998, 2002, and 2003 for both grade levels across the country. In 2003, 26 percent of students assessed performed below the Basic level, while 74 percent performed at or above the Basic level. Of the eighth graders tested, 32 percent performed at or above the Proficient level, and 3 percent performed at the Advanced level. In comparison, in 1992, 31 percent of eighth graders assessed performed below the Basic level, while 69 percent performed at or above the Basic level. Of the eighth graders assessed in 1992, 29 percent performed at or above the Proficient level, and 3 percent performed at the Advanced level. Performance at the Basic and Proficient levels increased slightly between 1992 and 2003, but only by a few percentage points.

The NAEP reading assessment measures students' comprehension of grade-appropriate reading materials that are drawn from sources available to them inside and outside their schools. The students read the selections and answer the questions, some multiple choice and some requiring a written response, to test their understanding.

Basic level is defined by the NAEP as the level at which students have partial mastery of the knowledge and skills needed for effective work at each grade tested. *Proficient level* represents solid academic performance for the grade assessed; students demonstrate their mastery of challenging subject matter and can apply their knowledge to real-world situations. *Advanced level* signifies superior performance.

In 2003 approximately 155,000 eighth graders from 6,100 schools in all fifty states were rated on a scale of 0–500; they needed a minimum score of 243 for the Basic level, 281 for the Proficient level, and 323 for the Advanced level. The average score of all eighth graders in 2003 was 263, compared to 260 in 1992. Although the increase may be considered statistically significant, it shows that our nation's eighth graders have not progressed in reading skills in the eleven years highlighted by the NAEP's report. In fact, eighth graders have not shown any significant increases in reading scores since 1998, despite such accommodations as extended testing time and small-group testing for students with disabilities and students with limited proficiency in English.

Girls scored better than boys did in each year of assessment from 1992 to 2003, with scores of eighth-grade girls as much as 15 points higher than those of eighth-grade boys in 1994 and no less than 9 points higher in 2002; in 2003 the gap was 11 points. White eighth graders scored slightly higher than Asian and Pacific Islander students, and both groups scored significantly higher than African American, Hispanic, and Native American students, but again the scores didn't differ significantly between 1992 and 2003, except for Asian and Pacific Islanders, whose scores declined. Eighth graders who were eligible for free or reduced-price lunches scored 25 points lower than those students who weren't eligible, but the scores didn't differ significantly from 1998 to 2003.

In the 2003 assessment, the percentage of Hispanic students participating rose to 15 percent and that of White students decreased to 63 percent, while the percentage of African American students remained steady at 16 percent. The assessment also revealed a significant gap in reading scores between eighth graders in public schools and those in nonpublic schools. In 2003 eighth-grade students in nonpublic schools had an average score of 282, with only 10 percent below the Basic level and 90 percent at or above the Basic level. Fifty-three percent scored at or above the Proficient level, and 8 percent were rated at the Advanced level. Eighth-grade students in public schools had an average score of 261, with 28 percent below the Basic level and 72 percent at or above the Basic level. Only 30 percent of the public school eighth-grade students scored at or

above the Proficient level, and 3 percent were rated at the Advanced level.

The report, published by the Institute of Education Sciences at the U.S. Department of Education, is not surprising but is somewhat disheartening and reflects Krashen's assertion quoted earlier.

The Programme for International Student Assessment, an international reading study conducted in 2000, assessed the reading proficiency of fifteen-year-old students in thirty-two countries. The report, *Reading for Change: Performance and Engagement across Countries*, was issued by the Organization for Economic Cooperation and Development (OECD). The fifteen-year-olds in the United States scored in the middle levels of reading proficiency in this study. Other key findings include the following:

Access to books at home is important.

Teens whose parents have lower occupational status but are enthusiastic and engaged in reading do better than teens whose parents have higher occupational status but don't engage in much reading.

Although teens who read a variety of printed materials are more proficient in reading, those teens who engage in "light" reading—magazines, comic books, and newspapers—do become proficient readers.[4]

A number of studies indicate that the summer setback, or gap, among children is real; reading skills do diminish over summer vacation, even for better students, although their skills don't decline as much as those of students who are already struggling. This summer setback widens the gap in achievement between lower-income and higher-income children. The New York State Library's Statewide Summer Reading Program website includes a document titled "Highlights of Research on Summer Reading and Effects on Student Achievement" (http://www.nysl.nysed.gov/libdev/summer/research.htm). Several studies discussing the achievement gap are summarized here, including *Building Effective Programs for Summer Learning* by Peter Johnson and "Lost Summers: For Some Children, Few Books and Few Opportunities to Read" by Anne McGill-Franzen and Richard Allington. Johnson notes that summer losses in achievement add up year by year throughout elementary school, while McGill-Franzen and Allington state that by middle school, summer reading loss produces a lag of two or more years in reading achievement.[5] In their review of two decades of literature exploring the effects of summer reading loss on the achievement gap between lower-income and higher-income children, Allington and McGill-Franzen found the research shows strong evidence that summer reading setback is one of the most important factors contributing to the achievement gap.[6]

THE EFFECTS OF SUMMER READING

In a 2003 study of a group of children who had just completed fifth grade, J. Kim found that those who read more over the summer gained in reading comprehension. Reading just five books over the summer caused a 3 percentile gain in reading comprehension.[7] Jim Trelease, in his *Read-Aloud Handbook*, states that the research on summer gap shows that summer reading—both to the child and by the child—helps to prevent that achievement gap. He also suggests that children join library summer reading programs.[8] Donna Celano and Susan B. Neuman, describing how public libraries help to foster literacy skills through summer reading programs, quote a librarian who said, "Parents have told me that their children's reading skills often improve over the summer months. Teachers have also told us that they can tell when children have participated in the reading club because they don't have to reteach what they learned last year."[9]

Celano and Neuman also compared the summer reading abilities of two groups of children in urban Philadelphia—children who joined summer reading programs at two libraries in highly urban areas of the city, and children who attended day camps in the city, located near libraries but with no reading programs. Both groups of children were racially mixed, with an African American majority. After the children had been attending the library programs and day camps for a few weeks, they were given two tests: the Johns Reading Inventory Test, which determines a child's instructional level of reading, and the Author Recognition Test, which measures how well children recognize famous authors and titles of books appropriate for their age level. Posttests couldn't be administered because attendance both at the libraries' programs and at the day camps was sporadic, and the researchers couldn't find the same children to test again. Despite this difficulty, the tests Celano and Neuman did administer showed that children who attended the library programs did better than the children in the day camps did. In the Johns Reading Inventory Test, the average grade level of children attending the library summer reading programs was third grade, and their average reading ability was 2.9, just a shade under their grade level. The average grade level of children in day camps was fourth grade, but their average reading level was 2.2. Neither group did very well on the Author Recognition Test, but the children in the library programs recognized double the number of authors and titles that the day camp attendees did (six authors and ten titles versus three authors and five titles; the test included twenty-five authors and titles). All the children in the study came from low-income, working families; all of them were reading below grade level, and none had much exposure to books outside the public library.[10]

The preceding studies all focused on elementary school children, not on young adults, but the research does point to the value of summer reading for maintaining reading abilities and preventing the summer setback. Krashen fully supports what he calls Free Voluntary Reading in school programs such as Silent Sustained Reading (SSR) and Drop Everything and Read (DEAR). Trelease also firmly believes in the value of SSR at school and at home. When children and teens are allowed to read what they want—books, magazines, graphic novels and comic books, fiction and nonfiction—they can improve their reading skills. As Krashen asserts,

> Studies showing that reading enhances literacy development lead to what should be an uncontroversial conclusion: Reading is good for you. The research, however, supports a stronger conclusion: Reading is the only way, the only way we become good readers, develop a good writing style, an adequate vocabulary, advanced grammatical competence, and the only way we become good spellers.[11]

WHAT ABOUT TEENS?

A 2001 article in *Publishers Weekly* summarized the results of a survey conducted for the National Education Association that indicated teenagers are reading more than some people think. The survey included 509 young adults aged twelve to eighteen. Of this group, 56 percent read more than ten books a year, and 41 percent read more than fifteen books a year. Middle school students read the most—70 percent of them read more than ten books a year—while 49 percent of high school students did so. When asked to describe reading, 87 percent of the young adults described it as "relaxing," 85 percent said it is "rewarding and satisfying," and 70 percent said reading is "stimulating or interesting." Forty-two percent also said they read for pleasure, not just for school. Minority students—Hispanic and African American—were more enthusiastic about reading than were White students, and minority parents tended to be more encouraging of reading than were White parents.[12]

Ken Haycock, in his "What Works" column for *Teacher Librarian*, summarized a few studies conducted around 2000–2001. A California study showed

- 64 percent of teenagers rated reading as a 7 or better on a "fun" scale of 1–10,

- 91 percent rated reading as "really cool" or "kind of cool,"

- 85 percent read outside of school,

- 58 percent said they read four days a week or more,

- 88 percent believed reading was "really important" for success, and

- 66 percent got their books at the library.

In a North Carolina study, 82 percent of teens said they read in their spare time, and 90 percent got their books from their school library. In a national SmartGirl survey of teen reading, 72 percent of teens said "I read for my own personal satisfaction" or "I don't have much time to read for pleasure but I like to when I get the chance." More than 90 percent said they read a book a month or more, and 62 percent got their books from the school library. Some teens claimed they don't read "except for comic books or magazines" or "romance, mystery, and scary books."[13] Apparently, many teens who describe themselves as nonreaders are, in fact, reading.

After a Kansas YA (Young Adult) librarian told me she accepted teens' reading of the backs of cereal boxes, I used that in my school visits to promote my library's YA summer reading program. I told teens that I would count time reading their email, newspapers, even the headline news on television. Middle school boys really picked up on that, and some of them did come into the library to register for the summer reading program. You can never tell just what might inspire a teen to join a reading program. After my library switched to counting time rather than books, it took me two years to convince one high school student that he could join the YA summer reading program, count the time he spent reading his email on the computer or reading the magazines he loved (he was a professional wrestling fan), and get free books. He finally joined during his last year in high school, although he was still skeptical until he saw we had included copies of pro wrestler biographies among the prize books. He put in enough hours to earn a book, chose his favorite from what we had, read that, and kept going. You can never tell. . . .

TEEN ALTRUISM— VOLUNTEERING IN THE LIBRARY

Despite the preponderance of media reports and articles focusing on teens doing bad, sometimes horrible things (such as the school killings at Red Lake High School in March 2005), lots of teens are actually doing good for their communities. In an article about teen volunteers, Paula M. White cites a survey done by Independent Sector, an organization in Washington, D.C., that tracks volunteerism. The organization surveyed one thousand teens in 1996 and found that more than one-third of them started volunteering before the age of twelve.[14] In another article about teen volunteers, Scott Poland cites a study by the Carnegie Foundation showing that teens succeed when they (1) have a sense of belonging at home, in their neighborhood, and at school; (2) perform three or more hours of organized activities each week; and (3) participate in volunteer activities to learn to focus on the needs of others.[15] *America's Teenage Volunteers: Civic Participation Begins Early in Life*, a booklet published by Independent Sector, states that in 1996, 59 percent of America's teens aged twelve to seventeen (13,300,000 teens) volunteered an average of 3.5 hours a week, for a total of 2.4 billion hours. In addition, 41 percent of the teens contributed to charitable organizations, averaging $82 each in 1995. Teens were nearly four times more likely to volunteer if they were asked; of those teens who reported being asked to volunteer, 93 percent did so. Of the 49 percent who said they were not asked, only 24 percent volunteered.[16]

Teens in the Library: Findings from the Evaluation of Public Libraries as Partners in Youth Development was published in July 2004 by the Chapin Hall Center for Children at the University of Chicago. Although the Wallace Foundation–funded program focused more on providing employment opportunities for teens in public libraries, five of the nine library sites in the study also formed youth advisory councils that advised library staff and helped to make decisions to improve library services for youth.[17]

In this book you will find descriptions of teen volunteers and variations of teen library councils at libraries all over the United States.[18] More libraries are working with teens and providing opportunities for them to actively participate in policy decisions, programming, and other activities to promote the library to young adults. Teen participation has been a major part of YALSA's mission. Harnessing the positive energy and enthusiasm of teens and preteens can energize librarians, too.

Why publish another book on summer reading programs for young adults? Because reading is still an important activity to help teens develop other skills, because there are teens who think reading is fun and libraries should continue to support that attitude, because libraries are a good place to provide avenues for volunteer and other community activities. The programs highlighted in this book show that libraries of all sizes and in all kinds of communities can provide meaningful and fun programs for teens, no matter the size of the budget. Librarians can choose elements they like for their own programs, and they may find new programming ideas to try with their teens. Whether you have been running summer programs for years or are just getting started, you will find lots of ideas here. Summers are still sizzling at libraries everywhere—yours can, too.

NOTES

1. Stephen Krashen, *The Power of Reading: Insights from the Research*, 2nd ed. (Westport, CT: Libraries Unlimited, 2004), x.
2. Patrick Jones and Joel Shoemaker, *Do It Right: Best Practices for Serving Young Adults in School and Public Libraries* (New York: Neal-Schuman, 2001), 103.
3. National Center for Education Statistics, National Assessment of Educational Progress (NAEP), *The Nation's Report Card: Reading Highlights 2003* (Washington, DC: U.S. Department of Education, 2003).
4. "New OECD Report Offers Insight into Adolescents' Reading Performance," *Reading Today* 20 (February–March 2003): 33.
5. Peter Johnson, *Building Effective Programs for Summer Learning* (Washington, DC: U.S. Department of Education, 2000); Anne McGill-Franzen and Richard Allington, "Lost Summers: For Some Children, Few Books and Few Opportunities to Read," *Classroom Leadership* (The Center for Summer Learning at Johns Hopkins University, August 2001).
6. Richard L. Allington and Anne McGill-Franzen, "The Impact of Summer Setback on the Reading Achievement Gap," *Phi Delta Kappan* 85 (September 2003): 68–75.
7. Cited in Krashen, *The Power of Reading*, 9.
8. Jim Trelease, *The Read-Aloud Handbook*, 5th ed. (New York: Penguin Books, 2001)
9. Donna Celano and Susan B. Neuman, *The Role of Public Libraries in Children's Literacy Development: An Evaluation Report* (Harrisburg: Pennsylvania Library Association, 2001).
10. Ibid.
11. Krashen, *The Power of Reading*, 37.
12. "Teens Are Reading Plenty, New Survey Finds," *Publishers Weekly* 248 (April 2, 2001): 23.
13. Ken Haycock, "Support Libraries to Improve Teen Reading (What Works)," *Teacher Librarian* 30 (February 2003): 35.
14. Paula M. White, "Straight from Their Heart," *Essence* 29 (April 1999): 146.
15. Scott Poland, "The Spirit of Giving Is Alive among Teenagers," *USA Today* (Society for the Advancement of Education) 131 (July 2002): 58–59.
16. *America's Teenage Volunteers: Civic Participation Begins Early in Life*, ed. Matthew Hamilton and Afshan Hussain (Washington, DC: Independent Sector, 1996).
17. Julie Spielberger et al., *Teens in the Library: Findings from the Evaluation of Public Libraries as Partners in Youth Development* (Chicago: Chapin Hall Center for Children at the University of Chicago, 2004).
18. Many of the programs described used or adapted the "@ your library"® slogan from the American Library Association's Campaign for America's Libraries. Phrasing and capitalization have been retained according to individual library usage. The official trademark use policy and instructions are available at http://www.ala.org/ala/pio/campaign/downloadlogos/use.htm.

READING INCENTIVE PROGRAMS

Some experts, including Alfie Kohn, have criticized incentive programs, saying children and teens should read only for the intrinsic rewards.[1] That works for avid readers who love books, but as Jim Trelease asks in *The Read-Aloud Handbook*, "If pure intrinsics is so successful, where has it been all these years? . . . How effective were the intrinsics if 60 percent of students found no pleasure in reading and didn't read much?"[2] Although Trelease was discussing electronic incentive programs such as Accelerated Reading, his questions also apply to summer reading incentive programs.

In January 2005 YALSA sent out a summer reading program survey to the main YALSA electronic discussion groups—YALSA-BK, YA-YAAC, and YALSA-L. The survey asked questions about what types of summer reading programs the libraries offered for young adults and about teen participation as volunteers at the library. The reading incentive program, wherein teens read whole books or a certain number of pages or hours and so on to win prizes, is still the most popular type of summer reading program, based on the survey responses. The programs ranged from statewide themes to independent local municipal efforts and from highly structured games to very informal clubs. Libraries from all over the country sent information about the programs they ran in 2004, and some sent their plans for 2005. Not every library gave information about funding, but if it was mentioned, that information will also be found in this chapter. Any brief mentions of programming and teen volunteer work are also included.

Another major difference between the programs discussed in the first *Sizzling Summer Reading Programs for Young Adults* and this new edition is the increased use of shared graphics and program ideas provided by state libraries, consortia, and collaboratives. I've noticed that a number of the programs in this chapter use such shared graphics and that this has encouraged many libraries to offer a young adult summer reading program. Such sharing means that libraries with limited resources can provide a fun and entertaining summer reading program for their young adult patrons without straining staff.

NOTES

1. Alfie Kohn, *Punished by Rewards: The Trouble with Gold Stars, Incentive Plans, A's, Praise, and Other Bribes* (Boston: Houghton Mifflin, 1999).
2. Jim Trelease, The Read-Aloud Handbook, 5th ed. (New York: Penguin Books), 128.

"Making Waves @ The Library"

North Liberty Community Library

North Liberty, Iowa

The North Liberty Community Library in North Liberty, Iowa, has run summer reading programs for teens for several years. "Making Waves @ The Library" was the 2004 theme. The teens who signed up were asked to read six books at their reading level during the six-week program. They kept track of their reading on a reading log. Those who completed the program received T-shirts and a $10 certificate from the local Applebee's Grill and Bar. In addition, teens could fill out a raffle ticket for every two hundred pages read or two hours spent reading. The library held one program each of the six weeks, leading to the finale, which was a pool party. Teens who read more than six books and attended at least one of the weekly programs could participate in the raffle drawing at the program's finale. Seventy-one teens (in grades seven through twelve) participated, and fifty-nine completed the program; thirty-five teens attended at least one program and read to earn raffle tickets. They turned in 320 raffle tickets and read more than 51,600 pages and 236 hours combined.

~North Liberty Community Library~
Teen Summer Reading Program 2004

Six local businesses (banks and private businesses) sponsored the T-shirts. Wal-Mart provided community grants for 2003 and 2004, and area businesses donated raffle prizes. The local cable company helped Assistant Director/Teen Librarian Jennifer Garner by designing logos, taping programs, and providing publicity. The cable company also made a DVD of summer program highlights to use in commercials for the 2005 summer reading program.

The Teen Advocate Group (TAG) helps Garner come up with ideas for programs, participates in the programs, and gives hands-on help when needed. In 2004 programs included Mehndi temporary tattooing, a Food Fear Factor event, and a photography contest (the latter two are described in the chapter on special programs later in this book).

Allen Park Public Library Young Adult Summer Reading Program

Allen Park Public Library

Allen Park, Michigan

The prosaic name belies a very active program that has run for five summers in Allen Park, just a few minutes' drive south of Detroit. For the 2004 program, "Get Lost @ Your Library," Young Adult Librarian Karen Smith set up a point system for the teens who participated. During the six-week reading program, young adults aged eleven through seventeen could earn points by reading, listening to audiobooks, volunteering, attending weekly events, and writing book reviews. The point structure was as follows:

Books	1 point per page
Magazines and Newspapers	40 points each
Volunteering	40 points per activity
Attending Program Events	30 points each
Book Reviews	20 points each
Member of Advisory Board	40 points

Participants needed to earn at least 1,200 points to be eligible for the Library Lock-In (see the Fun and Games section in the chapter on special programs later in this book). Teens who volunteered did such tasks as help with the children's programs, work in the library's gardens, and shelf read to earn their points. Twenty-six teens registered and eighteen completed the program. They collectively earned 45,089 points, which averaged out to about 2,504 points per teen.

The reading program began with a Kick-Off Party where teens registered for the program and the events they wanted to attend, and they received a point log, program guidelines, and admission tickets for each event. After registration, the participants were divided into three teams for a game of Jeopardy. Smith used sources such as the *Guinness Book of World Records, The Top Ten of Everything, The World Almanac*, the Jeopardy board game, and websites to develop questions. Each team chose a captain to ring the bell. Teams didn't lose points for guessing wrong, but each team was allowed only one guess per question. Each round included one Double Jeopardy question, picked at random by a library staff person. For Final Jeopardy, the teams selected two players who left the meeting room to find the answer in a library book. At the end of the game, each participant on the first-place team received 50 points, each participant on the second-place team received 25 points, and each participant on the third-place team received 10 points; these points could be used toward each participant's 1,200 points.

At the end of the six weeks, the library held a pizza dinner and awards presentation. Each participant who earned 1,200 points received a goody bag that included a pencil, bookmark, stickers, and book. In addition, other prizes were awarded to the teens who earned the most points. In 2004 one teen earned 12,958 points for the top score. The library ordered some prizes from Highsmith, and businesses and the Detroit professional sports teams—the Red Wings (hockey), the Lions (football), the Pistons and the Shock (basketball), and the Tigers (baseball)—donated prize items.

The Young Adult Advisory Board offered suggestions about performers and prizes for the summer program. Smith also gave each participant at the Library Lock-In a survey about the programs and used the responses to help design the next summer's program.

Allen Park Public Library
Young Adult Summer Reading Program
GET LOST @ Your Library

Evaluation Form

Rate the Summer Reading Program on a scale from 1–10, with 10 being the highest.

| 1 | 2 | 3 | 4 | 5 | 6 | 7 | 8 | 9 | 10 |

Rate the following events on a scale from 1–10, with 10 being the highest.

BINGO

| 1 | 2 | 3 | 4 | 5 | 6 | 7 | 8 | 9 | 10 |

Magic Show / Workshop

| 1 | 2 | 3 | 4 | 5 | 6 | 7 | 8 | 9 | 10 |

Craft

| 1 | 2 | 3 | 4 | 5 | 6 | 7 | 8 | 9 | 10 |

Science Alive!

| 1 | 2 | 3 | 4 | 5 | 6 | 7 | 8 | 9 | 10 |

What would you like to see added to the Summer Reading Program?

What would you like to see deleted from the Summer Reading Program?

Other Comments?

"Discover New Trails at Your Library"

Bettendorf Public Library

Bettendorf, Iowa

For the 2004 summer reading program at Bettendorf Public Library, Young Adult Librarian Maria Levetzow and her Teen Advisory Board members used decorations based on an outdoors theme. Of the 465 young adults in grades six through twelve who registered for the program, 217 reached the halfway mark and 200 finished the program. Levetzow used a point system in her program—participants who earned 600 points received an award for making it halfway, and those who earned 1,200 points received an award for finishing the program. Participants could count pages (1 point each) whether they read a book or listened to an audiobook. Magazines and newspapers were worth 30 points each

(for a maximum of 300 points). In addition, participants could write book reviews for 5 points each. They could also earn 1 point for each minute spent reading or listening to an audiobook.

The Teen Advisory Board chose the theme and many of the events, which included a street dance, a poetry workshop, a Library Survivor game, and Fairieality (some of these are described in the chapter on special programs later in this book). Board members often helped run the events.

Bettendorf's Friends organization and a local hospital cosponsored the 2004 summer reading program.

Teen Summer Reading Club— Montgomery County Public Libraries

Silver Spring Library

Silver Spring, Maryland

Teens aged twelve to eighteen years could sign up at the library for the Teen Summer Reading Club and then read whatever they liked. They then submitted brief (two- to three-sentence) recommendations for the books they enjoyed, either on paper or online through a link on the library's teen web page. Each branch library had prizes for the participants, and at the end of the summer, the recommendations were compiled into a booklet titled *Teen2Teen: Book Recommendations by Teens4Teens*, which is printed and distributed during Teen Read Week. The library has published the booklet for several years.

In 2004 about 725 participants read books and submitted book recommendations; Librarian Susan Levine at Silver Spring Library estimated that about 500 titles were recommended (there were a number of duplicate recommendations from different teens). About 110 titles were included in the *Teen2Teen* booklet. The program ran for seven weeks, from mid-June through the first week in August.

The *Teen2Teen* booklet was a second-tier winner in YALSA's 2004 Excellence in Library Service to Young Adults Recognition Project. The son of one of the system's librarians designed the cover art for the 2003 booklet. For 2004 the library ran a poster contest, which is described in the chapter on special programs.

Friends of the Montgomery County Library, Inc., BAPA's Imagination Stage, Big Train Baseball, Chick-Fil-A, Jerry's Subs & Pizzas, the Karate Learning Centers, McDonald's, Montgomery County Agricultural Fair, and Pizza Hut provided program support and prizes.

The library also provided other programs for teens throughout the summer—a teen band concert series, book discussion groups, pottery demonstrations, teen mystery theater nights, paperback book exchanges, and a chocolate tasting. Teens at various branches also helped with signing up participants, organizing and counting prizes, placing stickers on summer reading list books, preparing posters and flyers for special events, providing crowd control and setting up meeting rooms for programs, distributing reading logs, showing teens the prizes they won, and participating in programs.

"Read into Action"

Tucson-Pima Public Library

Tucson, Arizona

The Tucson-Pima Public Library system has offered teen summer reading programs since 1995. The 2004 theme was "Read into Action," and the program ran from May 20 through July 17. About four thousand teens in grades six through twelve participated, according to Senior Librarian Mary McKinney. Teens who registered at any of the twenty-three library locations earned incentives for every four hours of reading up to a total of twenty-four hours. The library planned to increase the total number of hours to thirty for 2005, with incentives for each ten hours of reading. The incentives include free passes for local attractions and fun prizes chosen by a teen advisory committee.

The Metropolitan Education Commission has a Youth Advisory Council/Tucson Teen Congress, and about twenty teens from this group participate in a library advisory committee. They develop the theme for the summer reading program, choose the incen-

tives, and develop library skills questions that teens must answer as part of the program. All the publicity items for the 2004 program were bilingual (English and Spanish), and comic books appeared in the background art.

Pima County, the City of Tucson, Tucson Sidewinders, and Friends of the Tucson-Pima Public Library have all been longtime sponsors of the summer reading program. Local restaurants, the *Arizona Daily Star*, Borders Books and Music, and Barnes and Noble have also been sponsors.

Throughout the summer, the various branches offered programs such as an after-hours mystery night (described in the chapter on special programs) and a teen poetry night, and teens provided musical accompaniment to librarians' storytelling at "Jammie Time," an evening story time for children.

"Explore Other Worlds @ your library"

Peabody Institute Library

Peabody, Massachusetts

"Explore Other Worlds @ your library" was the 2004 statewide summer reading program theme for Massachusetts. The Peabody Institute Library provided a number of programs designed around the theme, including a reading incentive program called "Battle of the Books." Teens signed up to be on one of two teams, which competed to read the most pages. Both teams combined read 28,404 pages. The winning team was invited to attend the library lock-in at the end of the summer. Lock-in programs are after-hours events that can run for several hours in the evening, with activities for the teens.

The library's youth group helped to plan the entire program, including the theme, programs, prizes, and advertising. A smaller Summer Reading Committee of four teens and the Young Adult librarian, Melissa Rauseo, addressed the specific details. The teens created a public service announcement that was one of the major advertisements; a teen scripted the four-minute "infomercial," which had an all-teen cast and was pro-duced by the local cable company. The PSA was shown at the public schools and on the local cable access channel.

The teens also planned and ran the kickoff party, attended by twenty-four teens. A teen bartender created "mocktails" (nonalcoholic drinks) with recipes chosen by the advisory group, and teens ran a game called "Around the World Roulette." Local businesses (Target, Shaw's Supermarket, J. C. Penney, Banknorth, Fly Away Travel, and Metro Bowl) and authors Nancy Werlin and Laurie Faria Stolarz donated prizes for the geography-based game.

Other events during the summer included a Taste of India program with henna tattooing, enjoyed by twenty-six teens, and a program on space discoveries (including a chance to try on space suits), which drew forty-five participants. Twenty-two teens came to a game day with a pizza taste-off, a library I Spy game, and "Online Sleuths," a mystery game. Rauseo reported that the attendance at these programs was higher than the average attendance at other YA programs.

"Time Twister"

Kalamazoo Public Library

Kalamazoo, Michigan

Kalamazoo Public Library (KPL) Teen Services and the Teen Advisory Board have been developing the Teen Summer Reading Game for a number of years, and participation at the game has grown to include more than five hundred teens every summer. The 2004 game, called "Time Twister," was a board game designed by the Teen Advisory Board. Teens who registered would read and count the number of pages read; when they read enough pages to roll a die to play the game, they could go to the library with their game board and do so. The game board included bonus spaces ("1775—Help Paul Revere warn that 'The British are coming!': +25 pages") and negative spaces ("1977—Get caught doing 'The Hustle' in a disco: –25 pages") and five Nexus Points. At each Nexus Point, the teens earned prizes, including KPL items such as flip pens, backpacks, and book lights, and coupons for food items; at the final Nexus Point, teens received a free paperback book. At various points in the game, teens could also complete raffle tickets for prizes such as a Nintendo Game Cube, $50 gift cards to stores such as Best Buy, Target, and Barnes and Noble, a portable CD player, a DVD player, and an MP3 player. In 2004, 587 teens registered for the game and 301 participated; teens read 995,407 pages total.

The library held a Wrap-Up Party for everyone who participated in one of the Summer Reading Games; there were games for children and adults as well as the teens. The event included food, inflatable attractions, a dunk tank, a climbing wall, kiddie games sponsored by the Teen Advisory Board, Book Bingo for the adults, and the Teen Prize Raffle. More than five hundred people attended the Wrap-Up Party.

The Teen Advisory Board started the planning for "Time Twisters" in the fall of 2003. A portion of each Teen Advisory Board meeting was devoted to brainstorming ideas, fleshing out the highly detailed game mechanics, and deciding the backstory for the game. Kalamazoo Public Library's Teen Services Programming Budget helped to pay for the summer reading game, along with a mini-grant from the Friends of the Kalamazoo Public Library and donations from more than fifty local businesses. Teen Services' Lead Librarian Kevin King estimated that the library raffled off more than $1,000 worth of prizes at the Wrap-Up Party.

Teen Services is a very active department and provides an average of twelve programs each month for teens; programs during the summer included drop-in gaming and crafts. In 2005 one of the major events was an appearance by Chris Crutcher, whose novel *Whale Talk* was challenged and banned in several U.S. states, including Michigan. To show support for the author and his work, a number of public libraries have engaged him to appear. Another program for summer 2005 was a Photo Scavenger Hunt. Teens registered as teams at their libraries, and each team received a camera. On June 21, from 3:00 to 6:00 p.m., the teams scoured downtown Kalamazoo for a predetermined list of cool things. They used their cameras to take photos of their team members each time they found one of the cool things. When they finished finding all the items on the list, they returned to the central library for pizza.

Reading Incentive Programs

"Stampede to Read"

Newport Beach Public Library

Newport Beach, California

Newport Beach Public Library uses the summer reading themes determined by the library consortium to which it belongs to create its Teen Summer Reading Program. In 2004 the theme was "Stampede to Read," which used graphics of running horses and cowboy lingo in publicity items. The program ran from June 28 through August 20. Teens in grades seven through twelve could sign up and read books; for each book, they were asked to complete a book review form. The completed reviews were posted throughout the Teen Center during the summer. Every review turned in qualified as an entry for weekly drawings and a grand prize drawing at the end of the summer. Participants could also select a new paperback book as a onetime prize after turning in their first five reviews. In 2004, 266 teens participated, reading about 850 books during the program.

Young Adult Reference Librarian Melissa Hartson worked with the Young Adult Advisory Council (YAAC) to plan the program. The YAAC members provided prize suggestions, which included gift certificates for local stores, eateries, cinemas, and iTunes. Other prizes included T-shirts, flip-flops, gift basket assortments, journals, and magnetic poetry kits. The 2004 grand prize was an Apple Mini iPod.

Other city departments have donated prizes such as city T-shirts, mugs, and bags. Newport Beach Fire and Rescue has contributed grand prizes in past years, including a rescue boat excursion for the winner and seven friends.

Much of the programming in 2004 focused on the commemoration of the Central Library's tenth anniversary. At the big celebration, a local band comprised of teens played contemporary jazz and Latin and funk music, and a local author spoke at the teen night, which was part of the main event. Teens also volunteered at the library, working at the Central Library and in the branches. They helped with the children's summer reading program, registering children and giving out prizes.

The theme for the 2005 program was "Unleash Your Power—Read," with a focus on superheroes. The library held Teen Movie Nights, with superhero movies, and a Graphic Novel Discussion Program (through the California Center for the Book).

"It's All Greek to Me"

Orange County Library System

Orlando, Florida

The 2004 Teen Summer Reading Program was the first ever held at the Orange County Library System. Teen Program Specialist Danielle King reported that the 2004 Summer Olympics, which were held in Greece that year, inspired the theme. Aided by the library's Teen Voices advisory group, she put together a series of program events and book talks that incorporated challenges faced by the ancient Olympians, such as bravery and endurance. The events included the "Wacky Olympic Games," "Toga Party," "Teen Battle of the Bands," a "You Don't Know Jack" trivia contest based on the irreverent computer game, "Fear Factor," "Library Lock-In," and "Reading Marathon." King decided to not count the number of books or pages read, or do any counting at all; her program simply allowed teens to register and read what they wanted to. She reported that the teens in Orange County have a tremendous amount of required summer reading assigned by the schools, so she kept the library's program as open as possible.

The program was such a success that Teen Voices helped King develop the 2005 summer reading program, "Sink Your Teeth into Reading!" Teens aged thirteen through eighteen registered and read books. The library provided a reading list called "A MENU of Books," and the teens were encouraged to submit book reviews, which earned a spot in the "Reading Cookbook," a collection of the best reviews organized by "cuisine" (genre). The cookbook was distributed via the teen website after the summer program concluded and was available throughout the 2005–2006 school year. A "Teen Battle of the Bands" kicked off the summer, and there were lots of food-related events. The Orlando Magic professional basketball team, Planet Smoothie, Muvico, and Universal Studios donated prizes for the events. In addition, all teen participants were entered into the Crunch 'n' Munch prize package drawing; the prize package included various beach items such as a beach bag, a towel, gift certificates, books, and lots of munchies.

Teen Summer Reading Program

Boca Raton Public Library

Boca Raton, Florida

Boca Raton Public Library has been running its Teen Summer Reading Program for several years. The library doesn't use themes, but the flyers do include fun slogans; in 2004 teens could "Chill Out This Summer" with the reading program. Teens aged eleven to nineteen came in to the library to register, putting a slip into a drawing box and receiving a small incentive (purchased from Janway—in the past these have ranged from a yo-yo to a water bottle to a message magnet). For each book the teens read over the summer, they filled out another slip to go into the drawing box. They could also write a review, which entitled them to put another slip in the drawing box. Each week Teen Coordinator Shilo Perlman drew one or two slips from the box and the winners received a prize. The prizes were all gift certificates to local businesses and increased in value each week, starting with a $5 certificate for Jamba Juice and including stores such as Blockbuster, Circuit City, Muvico, Barnes and Noble, and the Town Center Mall. All entries remained in the drawing box for the whole summer, so the more the teens read, the better their chances were of winning a prize. The program counted any required summer reading the teens had to do for school. Registration started in early June, and the drawings were held weekly beginning June 21 and ending on July 26. At the end of the summer, selected reviews were posted in the teen area of the library's website. In 2004, 261 participants read 927 books and submitted 340 reviews in 2004.

Crafts programs were also offered during the summer and included tie-dyeing and painting a wooden stool. The library offered biweekly game days, providing board and card games for teens who dropped in. The library's year-round film appreciation classes also continued monthly through the summer; teens could watch a recent hit movie, enjoy pizza and soda, and discuss the film.

The Teen Advisory Board helped to choose the sign-up incentive and gave Perlman ideas for what prizes the program should offer in the drawings. The library is not allowed to solicit businesses for gifts, so the Friends of the Boca Raton Library helps each year by purchasing the prizes for the drawings.

In 2005 Boca Raton teens were invited to "Say Aloha to Teen Summer Reading" beginning June 2. Two winners were drawn every week for gift certificates, using the same procedures as in 2004. The library website's Teen Zone posted the 2005 program schedule and included a slide show of past craft activities, such as creating clocks using CDs (you know those ubiquitous AOL promotional CDs?), painting wooden birdhouses, and more.

Join the Teen Summer Reading Program!
Ages 11-19
Sign up at the Youth Services desk & put an entry into the drawing box. Then, for every book you read over the summer you get to put another entry into the box. Two winners will be drawn each week beginning June 21st.
You could win one of these gift certificates...
June 21 - Jamba Juice $5
June 28 - Blockbuster $10
July 5 - Circuit City $15
July 12 - Muvico $20
July 19- Barnes & Noble $25
July 26 - Town Center Mall $30
Co-Sponsored by the Friends of the Boca Raton Library
Registration begins Tuesday, June 1st.
Each teen receives a free prize at registration!
Boca Raton Public Library, 200 NW Boca Raton Blvd.
(561) 393-7968   www.bocalibrary.org

"Extreme Read" Summer Reading Club

Mastics-Moriches-Shirley Community Library

Shirley, New York

Mastics-Moriches-Shirley Community Library is located on eastern Long Island, a suburb of New York City, and serves a racially mixed and economically depressed community. The library serves as the community center, and the staff is dedicated to providing programs to enrich the community. Librarian Mary Maggio said that the idea for "Extreme Read" came from the popularity of extreme sports. The owner of a local surf shop loaned surfboards, a wet suit, skateboards, wakeboards, and some clothing that teens often wear for sports activities, and he helped set up the decorations in the Teen Department. The library also purchased a BMX bike and in-line skates to use as decorations, and these were auctioned at the end of the program.

Teens who registered were asked to read at least two books to participate in the program. They received two thousand Xtreme Read Bucks just for signing up and five thousand Xtreme Read Bucks for each book they read. Everyone who read at least one book by July 28 was invited to participate in the Extreme Library Survival Scavenger Hunt, which was held on July 30 and 31. Teens who read at least two books by August 13 were invited to spend their Xtreme Read Bucks at the Extreme Read Auction on August 17. They could earn up to a maximum of fifty-two thousand Xtreme Read Bucks to spend at the auction. In addition to the regular auction, which included many small items so everyone could win something, the library held a Chinese Auction for those who read ten or more books. The BMX bicycle and some other pricy items were auctioned in the Chinese Auction, which is a variant on silent auctions.

The library offered a plethora of programs for teens that summer, including a book discussion, a creative writing group, pretzel making, a disc jockey workshop, horseback riding, and an extreme makeover workshop. In 2004, 360 teens in grades seven through twelve joined "Extreme Read."

You're Invited !

Tuesday, August 17th @ 6:30 pm

**TEEN SERVICES
SUMMER READING
CLUB
AUCTION**

After you receive this invitation, please call
the Teen Services Department
@ 399-1511 x 365
to let us know if you will be coming so we
can have your read bucks ready for you to
spend at the auction.

You're Invited !

Tuesday, August 17th @ 6:30 pm

**TEEN SERVICES
SUMMER READING
CLUB
AUCTION**

After you receive this invitation, please call
the Teen Services Department
@ 399-1511 x 365
to let us know if you will be coming so we
can have your read bucks ready for you to
spend at the auction.

You're Invited !

Tuesday, August 17th @ 6:30 pm

**TEEN SERVICES
SUMMER READING
CLUB
AUCTION**

After you receive this invitation, please call
the Teen Services Department
@ 399-1511 x 365
to let us know if you will be coming so we
can have your read bucks ready for you to
spend at the auction.

You're Invited !

Tuesday, August 17th @ 6:30 pm

**TEEN SERVICES
SUMMER READING
CLUB
AUCTION**

After you receive this invitation, please call
the Teen Services Department
@ 399-1511 x 365
to let us know if you will be coming so we
can have your read bucks ready for you to
spend at the auction.

Mastics-Moriches-Shirley Community Library

"Reading Rocks"

Allen County Public Library

Fort Wayne, Indiana

Allen County Public Library (ACPL) has been running teen summer reading programs for at least twenty years; the Young Adults' Services Department of the Main Library, established in 1952, has existed as a separate YA department for more than fifty years.

The 2004 theme was "Reading Rocks," with a focus on music. The program was open to teens entering grades six through twelve and included teens who had just graduated from high school. When they registered, participants received a pocket-sized, folded reading record with five milestones, shown as stars. Each milestone represented four to six hours of reading. When the teens completed each milestone, they received a gift—a book; a Pizza Hut coupon for a personal pan pizza; a voucher for a ticket to attend a Wizards game (the local baseball team); a pass to one of several destinations, such as Ultrazone, Little Turtle Raceway (go-karts), Cosmic Bowling at Wayne Recreation Center, and other gaming places; or a fine reduction coupon good for up to $10 off fines on the recipient's library card. After completing all five stars, the teens received a movie pass. They could continue reading and for every two hours spent reading, they could earn raffle tickets for entry into a drawing for several Borders gift certificates.

In 2004, 5,476 teens registered for the program, and participants read for a total of 97,907 hours. The library system awarded 7,017 books and other gifts, and 2,230 movie passes were given to those who completed the reading record. A total of 12,296 raffle tickets were handed out (there was a limit of twenty per participant). The assistant manager of the Young Adults' Services Department, Ian McKinney, reported that the gifts most awarded were books, movie passes, and Pizza Hut coupons. Most teens who received passes requested the Little Turtle Raceway and Ultrazone passes.

Allen County Public Library receives major funding from the Foellinger Foundation, a local foundation that supports the Young Adult summer reading program every year. The foundation purchases most of the prizes and pays for a full-time summer assistant who works with the Branch Youth Services Coordinator as well as for several teen summer assistants who help run the summer reading programs at Young Adults' Services and one of the busier branch libraries. The Wizards

ticket vouchers have been donated by the team every summer. The ACPL board approved the fine reduction coupon as a onetime special for 2004.

In addition to the reading program, the library offered some systemwide programs, including a beading workshop, a program on makeup and skin care, a workshop on body image and art, a miniatures-painting workshop for gamers, video games sessions, a chocolates workshop, yoga for teens, and a zine workshop. Some branches offered local programming as well, such as book discussion groups. The library kicked off the summer with a Teen Band Showcase held at the Barr Street Market, downtown and close to the Main Library's temporary location (ACPL was undergoing a massive construction/renovation project). Four bands with teen members, a couple of rappers, a vocal soloist, and a vocal group performed on the afternoon of June 5, and 200–250 people attended. Teens could register for the summer reading program, and the library raffled off a cardboard stand-up of Buffy the Vampire Slayer. Access Fort Wayne, the cable access channel housed at the Main Library, videotaped the concert and edited it to two hours; the video aired on the channel, and a commercial company burned it onto DVDs, which the library gave to the performers. The total number of workshops and programs for the summer was 159, with a total attendance of 1,882.

A committee with representatives from Young Adults' Services (YAS) and several branches along with the Branch Youth Services Coordinator planned the summer's programs, with input from library staff. Planning began in the fall, shortly after the previous summer reading program ended. Librarians and YA specialists visited schools throughout April and May to promote the summer programs; many times, the Volunteer Coordinator went along, mostly to promote volunteer opportunities for teens but also to participate in the book talks. The Teen Advisory Board scripted and acted in the public service announcement advertising the summer reading program, which was shown on local television stations. At the end of the program, library staff members were encouraged to complete evaluations, which were used to plan the next summer's program.

For 2005 the summer reading program became the summer library experience. McKinney said that the decision to change the name came from the reactions of a number of teens. One teen put it this way: "A 'program' sounds like something my mom would go to. At church." The theme was "Retro*Active: 2005 Summer Library Experience." The graphics had a 1970s look, and many of the summer events had a "retro" theme or feel. The reading milestones required six hours of reading. Teen community volunteerism was also part of the Summer Library Experience: teens were invited to collect aluminum cans for Habitat for Humanity. Each library location that was open (two branches were closed for renovations) had collection bins that Habitat for Humanity volunteers emptied each week, and the library kept a running total of the weight of cans collected. Teens led workshops on activities such as Mehndi tattooing, crocheting, and origami. The library hired an artist in residence who offered three- to six-week classes and onetime workshops at most of the branches on "sumi-e style" painting, wet-on-wet watercolor technique, and drawing techniques.

"For the Future"

Sevier County Public Library System

Sevierville, Tennessee

System Director K. C. Williams reported that the Sevier County Public Library System offered a teen summer reading program at one of the branch libraries in 2004. The Kodak Branch Library program "For the Future" ran from June 11 through August 6 for teens in grades seven through twelve. Teens who signed up could read anything they wanted—books, graphic novels, magazines, pamphlets, even CD liner notes—and were asked to complete reading logs. Each log represented six hours of reading in fifteen-minute increments, and the teens were asked to note the title of whatever they were reading. Each completed log was entered into a biweekly drawing for prizes, and when a teen completed three logs, he or she was entered into the grand prize drawing for a DVD player. Twenty teens registered and participated.

The Kodak Branch also offered other programs for teens, including basic wilderness survival skills presented by rangers from Panther Creek State Park; Basic CSI—Crime Scene Investigation; a basic self-defense program conducted by the Sevierville Police Department (parental permission was required for participation in this program); a time priority workshop to help teens learn how to plan their time to make high school, college, and career easier to handle; a creative writing workshop; and a Game Day during which teens could bring in their favorite card and/or board games for a relaxing afternoon of games and snacks. The Sevierville Police Department also offered a tour of its facilities (parental permission forms were required for this as well as transportation to and from the police station). On August 6 the branch held a party to celebrate the end of the program, with pizza, movies, and the grand prize drawing.

Local businesses such as banks, movie theaters, video stores, and fast-food eateries provided funds or food coupons for the prizes. Library staff members thought that the 2004 program was very successful, and they expanded the summer reading program to all three branches of the system for 2005. They also

started a monthly teen club for grades six through nine, meeting on a Friday evening from 6:00 to 8:00 p.m. The programs have rotated among the three branches and have averaged eight participants.

"I Get My Brain Food at The Bob"

Robert Cormier Center for Young Adults, Leominster Public Library

Leominster, Massachusetts

The wonderfully named Robert Cormier Center for Young Adults, affectionately nicknamed "The Bob" by members of the center's Red-Eye Writer's Group, conducts teen summer reading programs. The 2004 theme was "I Get My Brain Food at The Bob," and the program was open to teens entering grades seven through twelve. The participants read books of their choice in as many genres as they wished, including manga and graphic novels, reading five books to complete each "brain food" card; books more than 250 pages long counted as two books. For the first five cards they turned in, they won prizes as well as a raffle chance to win one of the special "Brain Food" T-shirts at summer's end. Prizes included bookmarks, movie passes, candy, buttons, and paperback books. After completing five cards, teens could continue to turn in cards for more raffle chances and to compete for the "top three" reader spots. Teenager Jeffrey Smith, a member of the Red-Eye Writer's Group and a graphic artist, designed the T-shirts. The top three readers each received a shirt and a gift certificate (donated by local merchants); the names of twenty more teens were drawn to receive a shirt. The program ran from June 21 through August 6; fifty-two teens participated, reading 1,115 books.

Young Adult Services Coordinator Diane Sanabria reported that "many years ago" she chose to use raffles (for a grand prize or a series of decent prizes) because she was uncomfortable with the competitive, "the one who reads the most gets the most stuff" mentality of many children's summer reading programs. According to Sanabria, that competitive aspect rewards the same really good readers year after year and discourages many average or below-average readers who know they are doomed from the start in terms of winning a top prize. With a raffle, the more teens read, the more chances they earn, but it is still the luck of the draw. Sanabria said, "I don't think I've had a year where the top reader was the grand prize winner!" In the future, she would like to incorporate an "individual reading goal" to further encourage lower-level readers.

The Bob also offered teen crafts programs, conducted by an alumnus of the Cormier Center. Events included Fun with Beads, Collage Journals and Bookmarks, Make Your Own Cosmetics, Journals and Beaded Pens, and Soap-Making. Other programs included a couple of drop-in contests: "Unmask the Stars" used disguised photographs of celebrities, including the mayor of Leominster (who was happy to be incorrectly identified as Mel Gibson), and "Where Are You in Leominster?" involved teens in identifying photographs of area buildings and landmarks, shot by local professional photographers. Author Terry Farish led a Teen Writing Workshop for high school students; it was so successful that it became an annual summer program.

T-shirt design

"Teens Rock @ your library"
Hawaii State Public Library System

The Hawaii State Public Library System (HSPLS), with fifty-one libraries, is the only statewide public library system in the United States. Kapolei Library on Oahu is the newest branch and opened just a couple of years ago. HSPLS has run statewide young adult summer reading programs since 1993. The 2004 theme was "Teens Rock @ your library." The system developed the graphics and the basic outline of the program, and each library in the system ran its own program. The program ran for about five weeks, from June 14 through July 17, and the teens in grades seven through twelve who registered were asked to read at least one book a week in order to pick up the week's incentive. The system handed out a bibliography of books on the program's theme. When participants registered, their names were entered into the statewide drawing sponsored by Pizza Hut, which has sponsored the sweepstakes since 1993. At the end of the program, three names were drawn; the grand prize was a $1,000 shopping spree at the Pearlridge Shopping Center on Oahu, the second prize was a $500 shopping spree, and the third prize was a $250 shopping spree. Frito-Lay also provided food incentives to hand out during the program.

Because Hawaii is an island state, winners often come from at least one Neighbor Island (Maui, Kauai, Hawaii, Lanai, or Molokai). If a winner is from another island, the winner and one parent are flown to Honolulu and back for the shopping spree. Two of the 2004 winners lived on the Big Island (Hawaii)—an eighth grader from Keaau and a tenth grader from Kau; the third winner, a Hawaii State Library patron, was a high school senior from Oahu. On the assigned day, a stretch limousine picked up the three winners and one parent each for a ride to the mall, where the teens could spend their winnings. A total of 3,305 teens registered and 2,378 teens participated in the program, reading 25,514 books. According to state law, the library system allows all registered teens to enter the drawing even if they don't read a single book. There can be no requirements to enter a sweepstakes drawing. In past years, winners had read at least one book and usually several.

The system's Library Development Section submits grant requests every year to the Friends of the Library and the Hawaii Library Foundation to secure funding to provide speakers or other programs in the library branches during the summer. One year an *American Idol* contestant sang at some of the libraries. In 2004 musician Darrell Labrado performed (he's a hot young local musician from Molokai).

The 2005 theme was "Read a Movie," and Pizza Hut once again sponsored the statewide sweepstakes. (Sponsorship is a year-to-year agreement between the company and HSPLS.)

"LOL (Laugh Out Loud)"

Northbrook Public Library

Northbrook, Illinois

Youth Services Librarian Karen Cruze, who is the Teen Specialist, enlisted her Teen Advisory Board (TAB) to help her plan the 2004 young adult summer reading club; she used the children's statewide theme of humor, and they called the teen program "LOL." Young adults in grades six through twelve could join the club; individuals going into sixth grade could join the children's club if they wished. Participants could count minutes or books (which had to be at least one hundred pages) and received coupons to area businesses (one per visit) and a paperback book at summer's end. Teens who chose to read books could read any YA or adult books they liked as long as they met the page minimum; those who chose to count hours could read or listen to anything—they could read picture books to their younger siblings, web-based fan fiction, magazines, and so on. The library designed the coupons (approved by the businesses' local owners and managers who donated the food items) for McDonald's fries, Baja Fresh tacos, Great Harvest cookies, Steak 'n Shake shakes, Lou Malnati's mini pizzas, Dairy Queen cones, and Dunkin' Donuts doughnuts. Other area shops and businesses donated other prizes, so the library was able to give out twelve stuffed goody bags per week as prizes for contests and drawings. The 2004 summer contest was a joke contest, which drew a lot of participation. A total of 334 teens participated in the club, and they counted 2,049 hours of reading and 1,480 books; 144 teens came in for the six times required to accumulate all the prizes.

The TAB members helped decorate the Young Adult area with emoticon happy faces (the kinds of icons found in many emails) in mobiles and with jokes printed in funky fonts, and Bart Simpson and Alfred E. Neuman cardboard stand-ups. Cruze first worked with the TAB to plan and run the 2004 young adult summer reading club, and she reports it was very successful and rewarding to work with the teens. She worked with them again for the 2005 club, using the statewide children's theme of superheroes.

"'Toon Up the Heat"

Schaumburg Township District Library

Schaumburg, Illinois

The 2004 young adult summer reading program at the Schaumburg Township District Library was "'Toon Up the Heat," using cartoons for the theme. Teens going into grades seven through twelve could sign up at any branch library and receive a bingo card reading log. Each square had a book genre or activity. When teens read a book, they filled out a review to mark their square; then they could enter drawings for prizes such as gift certificates for food, books, or music. When they finished the activities and books in a row of five

squares for bingo, they could pick up a prize between July 12 and August 31. Everyone who finished the program received a tie-dyed T-shirt (designed by the Teen Advisory Board) and a voucher for tickets to a Schaumburg Flyers baseball game. Teens who completed the program also received three tickets to the community-wide Teen Invasion.

The Teen Advisory Board (TAB) chose the theme and was largely responsible for planning the library activities. TAB members also helped run most of the

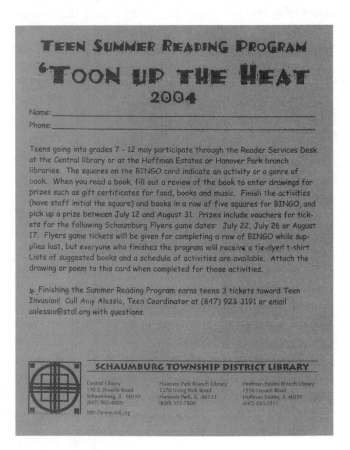

summer programs, such as the mystery dinner, the Summer Kick-Off Barbecue, scavenger hunt, and other activities. The barbecue was also the start of the Teen Invasion program and was held on June 18. Teens who attended the barbecue could earn their first Teen Invasion ticket.

Teen Invasion is a community-wide summer program for teens that started in 2003; the library is an integral part of the program. Teens earn tickets by participating in qualifying activities that help them learn about their community and channel their energy into many volunteer opportunities. Area businesses donate prizes for drawings held throughout the summer; prizes in 2004 included gift certificates to music stores and local shopping centers, passes to pools, movie tickets, and more. Beginning on June 14, teens could attend a Schaumburg Flyers baseball game, visit the Schaumburg Teen Center (The Barn), read a book from either the high school required reading lists or from a list of classics, attend a summer school class, visit a museum, register their bicycle with their local police department, or volunteer at the YMCA, the Schaumburg Township Spectrum Youth and Family Services Center, a Schaumburg Park District summer event, or any nonprofit agency. Each of these activities (and more!) earned tickets when the teens provided proof of their attendance or work (receipts, staff initials at the various centers, and so on), and those tickets

went into the drawings, which were held on July 2, 16, and 30 and August 13. A brochure explained all the qualifying activities and requirements.

In 2004 the program won the North Suburban Innovation Award from the North Suburban Library System.

The TAB chose "Slay a Book" for the 2005 Teen Summer Reading Event theme, which ran May 16 through August 31. Teens who signed up received a SCARE card (the bingo card), with the same procedures as in 2004. A plethora of library programs was offered, including the 2005 edition of Teen Invasion with even more activities than in 2004. Other programs included a Sisterhood of the Traveling Pants event with various craft activities for those who attended, including making jeans purses and friendship bracelets and making memorable journals; Terror Tuesdays, a weekly screening of horror movies; the Annual Mystery in the Library in which teens learn about what detectives do and then work in teams to solve a mystery (this event involved a small reservation fee); a Harry Potter Fest for kids aged ten and up; a Knit Wits knitting program; a workshop teaching the basics of anime and manga drawing styles; the Annual Road Rally hunt for clues and treasures in Towne Square; poetry and writing club programs led by a local author; and more.

"Discover New Trails @ your library"

Upper Arlington Public Library

Upper Arlington, Ohio

The Summer Vacation Reading Club at Upper Arlington Public Library includes all age levels from birth to adult. The library works with the schools for the children's and young adult programs. The 2004 club, "Discover New Trails @ your library," ran for nine weeks. Elementary and middle school students who signed up for the club counted hours read, eighteen hours being the goal for each participant. The schools competed for a trophy; all the students' hours were compiled for each school, and the school with the highest average number of hours read by each student won the trophy. Prizes were given at three different levels, and at the end of the program, the library held a drawing for the middle school readers; one girl and one boy each won a CD player. The high school program ran like the adults' program. Students turned in a slip for each book they read, and the library drew slips for prizes each week. At the end of the summer, all the slips were included in a grand prize drawing. The local high school has mandatory summer reading, so the public library works as a partner with the school; the Young Adult librarian and one adult librarian work with the teachers and students at the high school to develop the high school summer reading list, and the library purchases additional copies of the books listed. A total of 662 middle and high school students participated in the program; middle school readers read for 6,901 hours, and high school students read 1,352 books.

Teens also volunteered to plan and implement some of the preschool programs and helped at all programming events. They designed and ran a preschool craft and story hour all summer long. They were also encouraged to give suggestions for programming they would like to see at the library, which offered monthly book discussion groups and a wide variety of recreational and educational programs each week during the summer.

"Explore the Reading Trail"

Villa Park Public Library

Villa Park, Illinois

The Villa Park Public Library's Teen Summer Reading Club is open to participants in grades five through twelve. For the 2004 program, "Explore the Reading Trail," preteens and teens signed up at the library and received a booklet to record information about the books they read. They could choose one of two ways to keep track of their reading. For the first method, counting the number of pages read, teens received a booklet that included log sheets, with prize points at one thousand, two thousand, and three thousand pages. When participants reached each level, they filled out a short Book Response Form (essentially a brief book review), which they turned in for a prize. When they reached the three-thousand page level, they also received a raffle ticket for a chance to win one of the bigger prizes in the teen raffle held after the Summer Reading Club ended. For every five hundred pages they read after the first three thousand, they could receive another raffle ticket; there was no limit to how many extra tickets a teen could earn this way. There were also four activity sheets in the booklet (word search, match explorers with locations they explored, trivia quiz, crossword puzzle). Teens who completed all four earned an extra one hundred pages for their log.

The second method for recording reading was a bit more complicated but required fewer pages to be read to reach the three prize points. A "game board" (a two-page spread) was divided into thirty-six squares (six across, six down), each of which contained an idea for reading a different kind of book. For example, a square might say, "Read a book that makes you laugh," "Read a poetry book (or a novel written in poetry format)," or "Read a book about someone who survived a difficult time or event (fiction or nonfiction)." Each square also had a space to record the book's title, author(s), and number of pages. Participants could pick six squares in any direction and read six books to complete a line of six squares vertically, horizontally, or diagonally. They were required to read a different book for each square they completed; a single book could not count for multiple squares. The first goal level (equivalent to one thousand pages) was a completed line of six squares; the second goal level was twelve squares completed in two lines of six squares; and the third goal level was eighteen squares completed in three lines of six squares. A square in a completed line could be used more than once if it overlapped other lines. After completing the three rows of

Booklet cover, Villa Park Public Library

six squares, the teens could earn additional raffle tickets by reading five hundred pages for each ticket. They could also earn a free square by completing all four of the activity sheets.

For both methods, teens could listen to audiobooks and books intended for fifth grade and above; magazines didn't count. For the squares method, fiction books and illustrated novels had to be at least one hundred pages long, and nonfiction books had to be at least fifty pages long.

A total of 291 teens signed up; 126 finished reading one thousand pages or more, 100 finished reading two thousand pages or more, and 85 finished reading three thousand pages or more. Assistant Head of Youth Services Jean Jansen said that the library didn't keep track of the number of pages read beyond the three prize points.

Teens helped the library staff by working at the reading club's registration desk and awarding the prizes to those who reached the prize points. Teens who worked as library pages gave their input and critiques during the planning stages. The library sent out solicitation letters to local businesses and organizations in the spring requesting donations, and the library partnered with any businesses who wanted to help. Food coupons were all donated, either by the various businesses or through the Big Ticket Reading Program run by the *Daily Herald* (the local newspaper). Coupons for free admission to a matinee show were donated by the local movie theater. The library purchased books from Scholastic as well as some other, smaller prizes. The twelve raffle prizes included donated and purchased items, such as a DVD player; a pack with a beach blanket, swim goggles, a travel cup, and a light-up fan; a pack with a *Shrek* DVD, a *Shrek 3-D* DVD, and a *Shrek* tin with candy and microwave popcorn; a lava lamp; an electric personal organizer; a CD player with case; a *For the Love of the Cubs* book (about the Chicago Cubs); a one-year "Zoologist" membership to the Lincoln Park Zoo ($100 value) and a Lincoln Park Zoo T-shirt; one Family Pass (four admissions) to the Museum of Science and Industry ($36 value); a Polaroid I-Zone camera and sunglasses; a "Homemade Cookies for Dummies" cookie jar and a bag of cookie mix; and a blue basket filled with kiwi/melon-scented toiletries and three mesh bath sponges.

Other programs offered to the young adults included a monthly craft event, movies, and a murder mystery evening. The library also held many all-ages programs that some teens attended.

"Get Lost @ your library"

Natrona County Public Library

Casper, Wyoming

Young Adult Specialist Emily Daly reported that the 2004 theme for the Natrona County Public Library's teen summer reading program was "Get Lost @ your library." Teens signed up and read books, magazines, graphic novels, or whatever they chose in order to complete four levels. Each level required three books or three hours of reading, and teens could choose whether to record hours or books depending on how much of a challenge they wanted. They earned prizes for each level they completed, and for every two levels a teen completed, his or her name was added to a grand prize drawing for a $200 certificate from the local mall. Teens at the library suggested ideas for programs and prizes, and teen volunteers helped set up and tear down for the programs. A total of 496 teens registered, and participants read approximately 4,644 hours/books.

The Casper Rockies, a minor league baseball team, sponsored the programs for children and for teens. For every two levels of the reading program completed, teens (and children) received two free tickets for one of three special "Summer Reading Games." Teens and children who completed all four levels of the reading programs received four free tickets to be used at the special baseball games. McDonald's was another major sponsor, providing coupons for ice-cream cones, cheeseburgers, and extra-value meals for every level a child or teen completed; the restaurant also donated the $200 mall certificate grand prizes for both the children's and teen programs.

The library held "Drop In and Read" sessions every Thursday afternoon during the summer. Teen participants came to the library and read stories to children for one hour, and that hour of reading counted for both the teens and the children to whom they read. Some teens read one-on-one with a child, and some would read to small groups of children. Although very informal, the sessions provided opportunities for teens and younger children to work together.

The library also has two successful book clubs, one for sixth through eighth graders and one for ninth through twelfth graders, that each meet once a month during the year, including the summer months. Both groups meet at a local coffeehouse, and the library purchases paperback copies of the books being discussed for each participant as well as a drink or snack for each teen. The Anime Club meets once a month and is led primarily by high school students. The library also hosts at least one additional program per month for teens, such as Dinner and a Movie, Teen Mystery Nights, and workshops on makeup and skin care, applying to college, manga drawing, and more.

"Teens, Get Out of the Dark Ages: Read"

Danbury Library

Danbury, Connecticut

Teen Librarian Dymphna Harrigan reported that the Danbury Library's 2004 teen summer reading program adapted the Junior Library's medieval theme. The program ran from June 21 through August 28 and allowed teens to register and read any books they wanted, including any required summer reading titles. They could report as many books as they wished and as often as they wished, and they received one prize coupon per week as long as they reported at least once. Every Monday the library drew from the previous week's coupons, and three or more teens would win prizes. All coupons from each week were collected in a big box until the end of the summer, and then the library drew one grand prize winner from high school and one from middle school. The grand prize in 2004 was a trip to school on the first day in a limousine from Greg Scott Limousine, a local business. Other local businesses provided either prizes or funds to buy prizes for the weekly drawings. The Teen Council helped Harrigan select the theme once the Junior Library decided on their overall theme, and in 2004 senior members of the Teen Council ran the orientation for teen volunteers who worked at the library. A total of 124 teens registered for the program, and 63 of them reported books read; they read 297 books. Participation increased from 35 percent of registered teens in 2003 to 50 percent of registered teens in 2004, and the number of books they read more than doubled from the previous year.

The library also offered several programs throughout the summer, most of them for grades six through eight. A Harry Potter book discussion group met over four weeks throughout the summer to discuss the first four Harry Potter books, and then the Teen Council hosted a Harry Potter Trivia night. The Teen Council planned and ran the program and decorated the program room to look like the Great Room at Hogwarts. A local artist led teens through a craft program to create their own coat of arms; all participants also received tickets to the New York Renaissance Fair. The library also provided various opportunities for teens to volunteer. At the end of the summer, the library held a party for the reading program participants and teen volunteers. Along with food and drink, the teens enjoyed karaoke with the Spin Doctor.

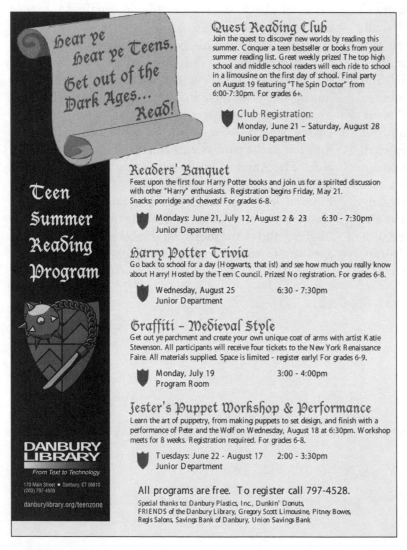

"Retro Reads"

Nashville Public Library, Hermitage Branch

Hermitage, Tennessee

DeAnza Williams, the Young Adult librarian at the Hermitage Branch of the Nashville Public Library, reported on the 2004 teen summer reading program, "Retro Reads." The program was held at all twenty-two locations of the Nashville Public Library. Teens aged twelve to eighteen signed up for the program, which ran from the beginning of June into mid-July. To finish the program, participants needed to complete three reading logs with space for six hours of reading on each, for a total of eighteen hours of reading. The reading logs became entries for biweekly drawings at each library location, including the bookmobile, and for the grand prize drawing. Upon completion of the three reading logs, the teens received a T-shirt, free admission to their choice of the local water park or the sports hall of fame, and a pair of tickets to the annual end-of-the-summer party, "Thursday Night Fever." They could continue to read and turn in more reading

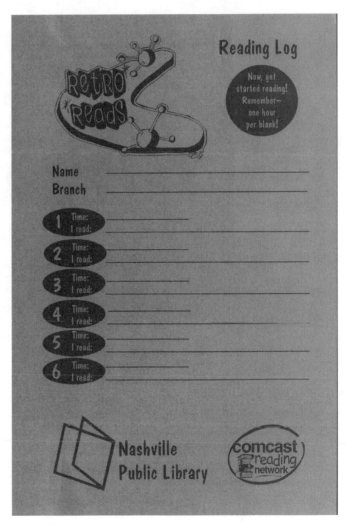

logs for more chances at the grand prize. The end-of-the-summer party included refreshments, karaoke, games, door prizes, a retro outfit contest, and the grand prize drawing. A total of 1,123 teens registered and 453 teens completed the required three logs; the teens spent 8,154 hours reading.

The Nashville Public Library holds a logo contest every year, and all teens aged twelve to eighteen who have a library card and live in Nashville are given the opportunity to design a logo for the teen summer reading program. The winning logo is used on all the promotional materials, including the gift T-shirt, and the winner receives a $50 gift certificate to a local art store. Teen Anna Thomsen won the 2004 logo design contest for "Retro Reads" with a design that looks like it came from *The Jetsons*, a television cartoon series from the 1960s.

Local businesses, such as malls, electronics stores, restaurants, other retail stores, and sports centers, have donated prizes for the biweekly drawings. The Nashville Sounds, the local minor league baseball team, also has partnered with the library for years, offering free admission to a game and a food coupon to children and teens who sign up early for the summer reading programs.

Many of the branches offered other teen programs during the summer, and the five regional branches and the Main Library had weekly or biweekly programs throughout the summer. Williams's branch, Hermitage, offered Totally Tie-Dye, where teens could tie-dye a T-shirt, socks, or shorts; Make a Groovy Lava Lamp (teens had to provide their own glass jar); Ice Cream and a Book discussion sessions on *The Outsiders* and *Fallen Angels*; a Marble Magnets craft program; a Retro Games night where teens played Twister, Connect Four, Monopoly, and other games with door prizes and refreshments; and a Retro Suncatcher craft program.

"New York Is Read, White and Blue"

Town of Ballston Community Library

Burnt Hills, New York

The Town of Ballston Community Library used the statewide New York Summer Reading Program theme for 2004, and Youth Services Librarian Karen DeAngelo adapted it for her teens. The teens who registered for the program read books, magazines, or comic books or listened to audiobooks (DeAngelo said she was even willing to accept emails, although no teen took her up on the offer), and every fifty pages counted as a book. The teens received book bucks for each book they read, and they could redeem those book bucks for prizes. DeAngelo purchased some prizes through Janway, which had custom-designed prizes using the statewide logo, and she asked local stores and businesses for donations; she accepted almost anything that could be suitable for teens, including nail polish and lipstick as well as food coupons. She sifted through all the donated paperbacks and pulled any that had teen appeal and were in excellent shape. In 2004 a woman donated sixty Beanie Babies, and DeAngelo said they were extremely popular prizes with all ages. All teens who participated in the VolunTeens program also participated in the reading program, so there were fifty-four readers. DeAngelo said she didn't keep separate records for reading by the VolunTeens, but they worked a total of 574 hours.

DeAngelo offered other programs, and she tried to have one per week during the summer. Her annual ductigami program is very popular with boys as well as girls. They make wallets, CD holders, and other items using duct tape. DeAngelo uses camouflage duct tape to make the wallets and says the boys love it.

In addition to the programs, DeAngelo offered many volunteer opportunities for teens in her library; these are discussed in the chapter on volunteering and teen participation later in this book. At the end-of-summer party for the VolunTeens, they made "kick the can" ice cream (put cream and flavorings in a small coffee can; put that can into a large coffee can and fill the space all around the smaller can with ice and rock salt; seal the can and roll it or kick it back and forth to make ice cream—it takes a while, but it is good). There were also prize drawings.

The 2005 statewide theme was "Tune In @ your library." DeAngelo had a local garage help her do a "tune-up" program, and she included music at the end-of-summer party. She offered a shekere-making craft program (a gourd rhythm instrument) as well as some passive crafts that could be left out on tables in the teen area with a teen volunteer guide/guard.

Teen graphic, 2004 New York State summer reading program

"Get the Arts in Your Smarts"

Southfield Public Library

Southfield, Michigan

Southfield Public Library's 2004 teen summer reading program was called "Get the Arts in Your Smarts" and focused on all types of arts, from the visual to the culinary. Teens in grades six through twelve who registered for the program were asked to complete three cards with different numbers of books to read and a corresponding creative activity to complete; each card required ten to fifteen hours of reading. When the teens turned in completed cards, they received a small prize and a raffle ticket for one of the three bigger prizes. A total of 180 teens registered for the program; 65 teens completed one card, 28 completed two cards, and 18 completed all three cards. The total number of hours spent reading was approximately 1,450. The

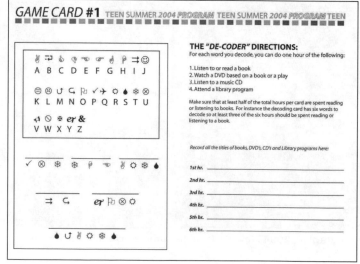

grand prize was a portable DVD player, the second prize was a digital camera, and the third prize was an MP3 player.

The library offered programs that tied into the arts theme: a cartooning workshop with a local professional artist; a program on quick cooking with a local caterer; Life of a Model with Sheryl Stokes of Barbizon Modeling in Southfield, who spoke about the real world of modeling; an open chat for teens about what they love and hate in television, movies, music, and other forms of entertainment; and Behind the Curtain with a speaker who talked about her experience as a radio DJ and about behind-the-scenes jobs in radio, television, and film. For this last program, teens also had the opportunity to work in groups to create their own commercials.

The Friends of the Library supported the summer reading program, providing funds to purchase the big prizes and allowing Youth Teen Services Librarian Shari Fesko to give coupons for free books at the organization's used book sales. The library's café also donated prize coupons.

For 2005 Fesko chose "DIY Summer" for the teen summer reading program theme and focused on all things do-it-yourself. Programs included Classic Cars: Nuts and Bolts, in which the owner of a classic car brought the car and discussed maintenance; Do It Yourself the Duct Tape Way; Room Revamp, with an interior decorator who gave advice on redecorating teen bedrooms; and a Use It or Lose It Do-It-Yourself Competition, in which teen contestants were given limited supplies and specific guidelines to create a functional item.

"Exploring Other Worlds"

Amesbury Public Library

Amesbury, Massachusetts

Each year, Young Adult Librarian Margie Walker and her teens use their summer reading program to make a difference in other people's lives. For Amesbury Public Library's 2004 teen summer reading program, "Exploring Other Worlds," the teens chose to support Heifer International. This organization asks people to help buy chicks, goats, rabbits, ducks, geese, and other animals that are sent to people in need in the United States and countries around the world. The idea is that when one gives food, it's a temporary thing—once the food is gone, it's gone; but when one gives an animal that can continue to provide food, the gift lasts much longer. A goat can supply a family with several quarts of milk each day, and extra milk can be sold or made into cheese, butter, or yogurt.

Participants used a bingo card to keep track of the materials they read. When they completed the required reading (spaces on the bingo card had such things as "Read a Comic Book," "Read a Non-fiction Book," "Read a Train Schedule"), they put an X through the box. When a row was filled, they received a raffle ticket for a chance to win prizes. All the prizes had a multicultural theme and included Worry Dolls, sweatshirts and T-shirts from Heifer International, items with an Irish theme, wood carvings from Africa, and so on. Walker wanted the teens to care more about the organization than the prizes. The Friends of the Amesbury Public Library funded the entire program. Eighty-six teens signed up, and they read a total of 1,256 hours. They were able to purchase ducks, a goat, a pig, sheep, and rabbits, which Heifer International donated to people in need.

The teens were involved in the whole process. They helped by copying the materials for the program, putting all the packets together, signing up teens, and explaining the program. They also monitored the hours that teens read, stamped logs, and gave out raffle tickets. Their work meant the library's staff members didn't have to take on the extra work of the summer reading program. Walker said that teen volunteers worked two-hour shifts and covered the entire fifty-eight hours per week that the library was open. Twenty teens were responsible for the summer reading program.

"A Century of Stories: One Hundred Years, Hundreds of Books"

Carmel Clay Public Library

Carmel, Indiana

The city of Carmel Clay is just north of Indianapolis. The Teen Library Council (TLC) works with Young Adult Services Manager Hope Baugh to organize the program each year, and for 2004 they tied the program to the library's yearlong centennial celebration. Members of the TLC dressed up in period costumes and posed for photos as people reading through the decades. The photos were used for a banner and other publicity materials for the program, which ran from June 7 through August 7.

Teens going into grades six through twelve registered and read whatever they liked (recording the number of pages read on their reading log). They earned Book Bucks they could redeem for prizes ("Summer Souvenirs") and raffle tickets for "Decade Drawings," which were held twice every week. Every fifty pages earned a Book Buck, and one hundred pages earned a Summer Souvenir, for a limit of two prizes. After the teens received their Summer Souvenirs, their Book Bucks served as raffle tickets. Summer Souvenirs included such items as crocheted hacky sacks, "Gooey Guys" putty, nine-piece tool chests, stretch watches, battery-operated handheld fans, inflatable cows, armband tattoos, flashlight fish key chains, cuddle bears, and "little people" key chains.

The Decade Drawings prizes were mostly gift cards from local businesses, loosely related to things that were invented during each of the decades that the library had been in existence. For example, for the week of June 13, the decade covered was 1904–1914. The first nickel theater (called a "nickelodeon") opened in 1905, so the prize was a $20 Regal Village Park Cinema gift card. Theodore Roosevelt was elected to a full term as president in 1904, and teddy bears became popular; the second prize that week was a $20 gift card to Kohl's department store. The library also raffled some cardboard stand-up figures from *The Lord of the Rings* for the week of July 18, which covered the sixth decade, 1954–1964; J. R. R. Tolkien wrote *The Lord of the Rings* books during that decade. Teens could earn extra raffle tickets by writing book reviews as well, which the library posted on its website (http://www.reads4teens.org).

When teens reached one thousand pages read, they could choose a paperback book from "The Book Vault" to keep and received a coupon for a free drink from Johnny Java, the library's coffee shop, as a completion prize; they were also able to continue reading as much as they liked to earn more raffle tickets. Teens could also read from a certain list of books for the "Quality Challenge" drawing for a "huge container of '100 Grand' candy bars" and/or read ten thousand pages for the "Quantity Challenge" drawing for another huge container of candy bars. The Friends of the Carmel Clay Public Library paid for almost all the prizes. A total of 1,024 teens participated in the Young Adult Summer Reading Program, and they read a whopping 1,806,742 pages. Of the participating teens, 527 reached the "completion goal" of one thousand pages.

1960s reader, Carmel Clay Public Library

1980s reader, Carmel Clay Public Library

The structure of the program and the kinds of prizes offered were based on the evaluation of the 2003 young adult summer reading program. Teens had said they wanted somewhat larger prizes rather than "a lot of little trinkety things," so the library offered the Summer Souvenirs. Teens also wanted more drawings for gift cards (again, rather than a lot of little prizes), so the library offered two Decade Drawings each week. The "Quantity Challenge" and "Quality Challenge" both had candy prizes, because teens said they wanted candy as one of the prizes.

Young Adult Services provides a number of clubs that meet regularly throughout the year, including the summer months: Graphic Novel Discussion Group, Mother-Daughter Book Discussion Group, Made into Movies, Anime Club, Art Attack, Origami Club, and Teen Library Council. The library has also offered one-time programs based on interest and opportunity.

In addition to the Teen Library Council, which actively works with Baugh to plan and implement all kinds of programs, the library has a Teen Volunteer Corps open to anyone going into sixth through twelfth grades. These are ongoing groups throughout the year.

"New York Is Read, White and Blue"

Saugerties Public Library

Saugerties, New York

The historic town of Saugerties, ninety miles north of New York City, uses the New York State Summer Reading Program theme each year. In 2004 the theme was "New York Is Read, White and Blue." Participating teens earned 100 points by reading, writing book reviews, completing puzzle pages, making illustrations, and doing other activities. Once they reached 100 points, they were entered into a drawing for prizes such as mall certificates, movie tickets, jewelry, books, and so on. Youth Services Clerk Stephanie McElrath reported that twenty-five teens completed the program, reading 211 books. Local businesses Smith Hardware, Tiffany Toys, Frank's Hunting Lodge, Dallas Hot Wieners, Exchange Hotel, Freedom Hair, Stella's Station, Trillium, YaYa Emporium, and Gristmill Real Estate supported the young adult program.

The library held one special program in the summer—poet John Heaviside led a poetry workshop at the Saugerties Public Library's Young Adult Poetry Café. He taught nine young poets to employ imagery in their creations, then each performed his or her expressive works for an audience. The local newspaper sent a photographer to capture the evening on film and published some photographs in the paper.

"Say What?"

Howard County Library, Glenwood Branch

Cooksville, Maryland

Teen Specialist Kris Buker reported that her library participated in the 2004 Teen Summer Reading Game tied into the statewide Maryland "Say What?" program. Baltimore County Public Library created the game and game board, as it does every year. The children's summer reading theme was "Readers Rule" with fairy-tale activities; the teen game incorporated fractured fairy tales, and many libraries played into the popularity of the animated film *Shrek 2*.

Teens aged eleven and up were invited to register for the game and received a four-page, folded game board with a fire-breathing dragon on the cover. There were twelve activities on the board, four of which were based on reading books in several different genres (science fiction/fantasy, nonfiction, and a biography). Other activities encouraged teens to "find out more @ your library" as well as by searching on the Internet for information; still other activities involved poetry, journals, and magazines or newspapers. Participants were asked to complete three activities to turn in a coupon and earn prizes. If all twelve activities were completed, participants' names were entered into a drawing for larger prizes. The program ran from June 1 through August 21. A total of 2,753 teens signed up at the beginning of the summer. Although the game required reading only four books, many teens completed only the activities that didn't require reading, even when Buker tried to encourage participants at her branch by telling them that graphic novels counted as nonfiction books. The library did encourage teens to read after they completed the game board's twelve activities; for every four additional books they read, they were entered again into the grand prize drawing. They could do this twice, for a total of three chances in the drawing. Many teens in the game did read the additional books and read even more than the total of twelve (four in the game and eight extra).

The library system purchased small prizes: key chains, highlighters, pens, notepads, playing cards, and bouncing balls. Teen Advisory Boards at several of the branch libraries helped library staff select the prizes, and these were given out when the participants turned in their coupons after finishing three activities. In 2004 one of the new movie theaters in town donated a pair of tickets to each of the six branches, and a local businessman donated his limousine service for the winners to ride to the theater. The Mall in Columbia (also in Howard County) donated a $125 gift card, which was the grand prize. Each branch also received two passes to Medieval Times, a family pack of tickets to attend a Frederick Keys baseball game (a minor league team of the Baltimore Orioles), a $15 gift card to Target, a $20 Outback Steakhouse gift card, and gift certificates to local sporting arenas (a baseball batting cage, roller skating rinks, and water centers). Some of these prizes were donated, and some were purchased by the library system.

In addition to the Teen Advisory Boards, other teens volunteered to help with the children's reading game, registering children, giving out prizes, creating crafts, and helping with some of the children's programs. Each of the branch libraries also offered teen programs; they offer programs throughout the year, and for the summer they had craft programs (tie-dyeing, stamping, cross-stitch and needlepoint, and decoupage), drop-in game nights, book clubs, ice-cream and pizza tasting, and more. Buker offered two Harry Potter trivia programs for kids aged eight and up, one around the time of the release of *Harry Potter and the Prisoner of Azkaban* and the other on Harry's birthday (July 31).

SUMMER 2004

Say What?

What Teens Want to Know

Were Dragons Dinosaurs?

The Godfathers of the Fairy Tale

The Blogging Fad:
Princess Diary Updated

High-Tech Search for Lost Treasures

Bestiary:
A Who's Who of Medieval Monsters

Game board, Howard County Library

"Book Your Summer!"

Washington Public Library

Washington, Missouri

Washington Public Library has held a young adult summer reading program for about five years; it's a ten-week program, run in conjunction with the library's adult and children's summer reading programs. Teens entering grades seven through twelve (or at least twelve years old) can join the program. For the "Book Your Summer!" reading program in 2004, teens were asked to complete four cards with four hours of reading on each card. They could read any library materials and their personal comics, if they had them. When they completed each reading card, they received small prizes, such as mood pencils, crazy pens (a big hit), small puzzles, gummy pizzas, marabou pens, bouncing balls that light up, and magnetic sculpture. When participants completed the four cards, for a total of sixteen hours, they were entered into a drawing held at the end of the program. The grand prize in the drawing was a CD boom box, and there were other prizes as well, including neon lamps in fun shapes (cactus, flamingo, palm tree, and so on) journals, and glass and marble chess sets. Library Director Carolyn Witt said she worked with the library's Teen Advisory Board to select prizes for the program. A total of 105 teens signed up for the program, and 39 reached the sixteen-hour goal; the participants read a total of more than seven hundred hours.

Young Adult Reading Club

Gail Borden Public Library

Elgin, Illinois

Youth Services Librarian Lisel Ulaszek reported that in 2004 teens could sign up for the Young Adult Reading Club (YARC) online or in person. The library didn't restrict participation, so teens from outside the library district could join. At sign-up, teens received a reading log; they then read materials of their choosing for twenty hours. Allowed materials included magazines, comics, graphic novels, audiobooks, fiction, and non-fiction. When the teens completed twenty hours, they brought their reading log to the library and received an entry into the drawing for the grand prize: a young adult book of their choice to keep, a movie pass donated by Classic Cinema 12, a pass to the end-of-YARC Survivalist Party, coupons from local businesses, and their choice of a "Big Ticket." The Big Tickets were free admissions to area attractions, including Medieval Times, free gaming at GameWorks or Laser Quest, a free ticket to a Chicago Wolves game, a free game of mini-golf at a local attraction, and others; these were all donated by the *Daily Herald* newspaper. Teens could complete more than one reading log if they wished, and they received an additional prize drawing slip for each reading log completed. At the YARC Survivalist Party, the library served food and drinks and held the prize drawings, and the teens played a version of the board game Worst-Case Scenario Survival Game. A total of 395 teens signed up for the summer reading program, and 167 of them completed the program. Each teen read for at least twenty hours; some teens (Ulaszek estimates twelve to fifteen) completed two reading logs, reading for a total of forty hours each.

In addition to the Big Ticket donations from the *Daily Herald*, a library staff member contacted local businesses to ask for donations—coupons for free coffee, free sandwiches, free games of bowling, and other items. Teens helped the library staff with the children's summer reading program; they manned the summer reading booth and helped children sign up, listened to them give their book reports, stamped reading logs, and helped give out prizes.

The library offered four teen programs called Teen Scene, two in June and two in July, that were open to teens entering grades seven through twelve; participants did not have to be members of the Young Adult Reading Club to attend these programs. The 2004 programs included a workshop where teens could make their own soaps and other beauty products; a comic book art workshop with artist Scott Beaderstadt; a stage improv class with staff from a local theater teaching how to do safe stage combat; and a rubber stamping workshop where teens could design their own notepads, note cards, and bookmarks.

"Read around . . . Florida"

New Port Richey Public Library

New Port Richey, Florida

Youth Services Librarian Tracey Pinto had tried more formally structured teen summer reading programs in years past, but she found they were poorly attended. She started running a very informal program that didn't require registration and found that more teens participated. In 2004 Pinto used the statewide summer reading theme "Read around . . . Florida" and set out ballot boxes and forms in high-traffic areas. Teens and tweens could simply fill out a form with their name, age, phone number, the title of the book, and a short review and drop it in the box as an entry into a prize drawing. They could read as much as they liked, and each entry form with a review gave them more chances to win. The program ran for two months. Local businesses such as Outback Steakhouse, Regal Cinemas, Wal-Mart, Target, Pizza Hut, golf courses, arcades, and sports teams all donated prizes for the program.

The library did have an active teen volunteer program during the summer. Teens helped the younger children during their reading program—they listened to the children read or read to them, they helped with the weekly projects, and they helped with other programs for elementary and middle school children. In addition, the library's Teen Advisory Club met twice a month, including the summer; they brainstormed programs they'd like to do, selected materials for the YA section, and discussed current events.

"Get Lost @ your library"

Plymouth District Library

Plymouth, Michigan

Teen Services Librarian Cathy Lichtman chose to use the 2004 state summer reading theme, "Get Lost @ your library," at Plymouth District Library, situated between Ann Arbor and Detroit, Michigan. Teens who signed up received a reading log and could choose either to read four books or to read three books from at least two different genres—graphic novels and audiobooks were also allowed—and complete one of several activities: read for one hour to a sibling or other younger child, attend a library program, or run, swim, or bike for one mile. When participants turned in a reading log, they received a free paperback book and were entered into the weekly drawing. If they completed and returned four reading logs, they received a pair of tickets to the AMC Movie Theaters. Teens could also enter the weekly drawings each time they attended a library program. Lichtman allowed teens to register at the library or online; she simply transferred the information from online registrations onto the cards. Teens turned in 386 reading logs; 135 teens turned in completed logs and received their free paperback books, and 60 turned in a total of four logs each and received the movie tickets. Lichtman didn't keep track of the nonreading activities, but she remembers that a lot of teens chose one of the activity options.

Weekly drawing prizes included coupons for ice cream, pizza, haircuts and manicures, skating, and laser tag. All the entries were put into the drawing for the grand prize, which was a $100 gift certificate to the local mall. Lichtman purchased small prizes with the state theme's logo from Highsmith and requested donations from local businesses; the Friends group at Plymouth also provided funds for prizes. The Teen Advisory Board helped Lichtman choose prizes, decide on the procedures, and plan programs.

During the summer, Lichtman offered a number of programs. She started the summer reading program with a Mystery Program and fed the teens pizza and ice-cream bars. Eric Kramp, husband of one of the librarians, led a three-session GURPS role-playing game; Michigan comics creator Jane Irwin (writer of *Vogelein: Clockwork Faerie*) conducted a mini comics workshop; and the library showed weekly movies on Wednesday nights. Craft programs included wearable art, beads, scrapbooking, making picture frames, and "doing your own thing." For the last event, Lichtman supplied materials such as duct tape and candy wrappers to make bracelets (the teens ate the candy) and hemp and beads for jewelry; teens signed up to teach their favorite craft. The final program was an after-hours party with the grand prize drawing, pizza, star scramble, an icebreaker, a movie, and board games and Mehndi tattooing for those who didn't want to watch *The Return of the King*.

Teen Library Programs at the Plymouth District Library

Mystery & Pizza Party –Monday, June 21 at 6 pm
"Death Gets a Red Card" - Sign up & get your character's information.

Mini Comics Workshop with Jane Irwin, Author of Vogelein, Thursday, July 15 at 6:30

Movie Nights—Wednesdays at 7 pm — Come hangout at the library with your friends. We'll supply the movie, popcorn and pop.
PG & PG-13
6/23, 7/7, 7/14, 7/21, 7/28, 8/4
**ANIME NIGHT **Wed. 6/16 at 6:30

GURPS* Role Playing Games with Eric Kramp
Wednesdays July 14, 21, 28 at 6:30 pm
*Generic Role Playing Systems

D.I.Y. D.I.Y. D.I.Y.

Wearable Art —Tuesday, June 15 at 3 pm—Bring items like t-shirts, flip flops, caps and sunglasses to decorate.

Do Your Own Thing—Saturday, July 10 at 2:30 pm—Tell us the craft you want to share and we'll buy the materials and photocopy instructions. Ideas: Starburst necklaces, hemp jewelry, duct tape wallets, friendship bracelets...

Beads, Beads, Beads —Monday, July 19 at 3 pm

Frame Up —Saturday, July 24 at 2:30–Create Frames for your favorite photos

Scrapbooking— Monday, August 2 at 3 pm—Bring 8—10 photos that fit together like friends, summer vacation, a holiday, family.

Speaking of Books

Books & Bagels—Monday, July 12 at 3:30 pm
    Monday, August 9 at 3:30
More B & B — Tuesday, June 20 at 3:30
SciFi Reads — Monday, June 28 at 3:30
    Monday, July 26 at 3:30

Sign-Up for End of Summer After Hours Pizza Party
Make your won sundaes
Fri. Aug. 6 ~ 6 - 11 pm
Games and a Movie
Grand Prize Drawing

Remember, there's always FOOD at all Teen Programs !

For more information or to sign up for any of these programs, stop by the Reader's Advisory Desk or call (734) 453-0750 and press 4.

2004 Teen Summer Reading Plymouth District Library June 14 – August 6, 2004

1. REGISTER at the library on or after June 12.

2. *GET LOST IN SOME GREAT BOOKS!*

3. Bring your completed reading log to the library and get a paperback book and a chance at the weekly prize drawing and the grand prize.*

4 * You can only win one paperback but, the more you read, the more chances you have to win movie tickets, weekly prizes and the Grand Prize!

Read 3 books from at least two Different Categories
(or read for 12 hours)

Read an action or adventure book (ADV)
Get lost in a mystery or thriller (MYS)
Get lost in a graphic novel (GN)
Get lost in historical fiction (HIST)
Get lost in scifi/fantasy (SCIFI)
Get lost in romance book (ROM)
Get lost in realistic fiction (REAL)
Get lost laughing (FUN)
Get lost in non fiction or biography (NONFIC)
Get lost in a book on tape or cd (AUDIO)

And do one of these activities: (check one)

Read for 2 hours to a younger child _____

Attend a library program _____

Volunteer at the library for 2 hours _____
 Call Cathy Lichtman at 734-453-0750, ext. 230 to arrange

Get lost running, swimming or biking 2miles _____

OR

Read one more book _____
      Title

_____
      Author

Title	Author	Category
Title	Author	Category
Title	Author	Category

OR check a box for each hour spent reading
فَاقِف آف فَاقِف آف
AND

Activity _____

- -

Name _____

Address _____

City _____ Phone _____

School _____ Grade _____

Turn in your completed form for a free book and a chance to win the weekly prize and the Grand Prize., $100 gift certificate to Twelve Oaks Mall.   You can only win one book but additional forms can be turned in for the Weekly Prize and the Grand Prize drawings. Complete and turn in 4 forms, and you will receive a pair of movie tickets to a local theater.

Date turned in _____

"Stampede to Read"

Upland Public Library

Upland, California

The Upland Public Library in San Bernardino County in Southern California has held teen summer reading programs since 1997, said Randee Bybee, library assistant in Children's Services. In 2004 teens signed up and were asked to read six books they had never read before, over a seven-week period. When they signed up, they received a full-color, theme-related diary in which they were to record the titles and authors of the books they read. They wrote their name on a clipboard and received a number that would be theirs for the duration of the game. They also received a free paperback book; each week when participants came to the library with diaries in hand and checked in, they received a vendor coupon for free food or activities. The teens had to check out books from the library to read for the program, and the books had to be at their reading level. At the end of the program, those teens who read six books received a $5 gift card to Borders Books and Music. Library staff tried not to police the program too much and relied on the teens' honor, but they held back the gift cards until the fourth week of the program to discourage "quick" readers. A total of 278 teens participated in the program, and 109 earned the Borders gift cards; Bybee reported that the number of participants increased substantially from the 170 teens who participated in 2003.

Local businesses and food vendors provided the coupons, which included food items such as tacos and personal pan pizzas and activities such as bowling and golf. The local Friends of the Library organization provided money for the Borders gift cards and the paperback book giveaway (the Friends group provides funding for all the teen programs at the library). The library purchased books from the local Scholastic book warehouse (Bybee reports they have some great discount bins) and from Foozles Discount Book Store. The Teen LAB (Library Advisory Board) helped to choose new vendors for the prizes.

Teens volunteered at the library and helped to conduct the children's summer reading program. For the children's program, the library created a game board similar to that for Monopoly, and the teens helped participants move along the board. Bybee noted that the children understood how the game worked, but the parents needed help. The Teen LAB assisted in presenting programs for teens. Each summer the library offers three special programs just for teens. Past programs have included making Butt Pillows (cut off the legs of old jeans, sew the openings closed, decorate, and stuff). In addition, a cartoonist visited, a museum curator brought in various Egyptian artifacts, the library hosted several mysteries, and a local college comedy improv group performed.

Upland Public Library

Teen Summer Reading Program

Benicia Public Library

Benicia, California

In 2004 Teen Services Librarian Kate Brown held the Teen Summer Reading Program from June 7 to August 20 at Benicia Public Library, in the Bay area near San Francisco. Teens aged thirteen through nineteen who signed up for the program read books, filled out forms—including a brief review of the books—and dropped the forms into a box in the Teen Section. Prizes were awarded based on the number of pages read, with prize points at 200, 400, 800, and 1,200 pages. The library held weekly drawings, and everyone who read at least one thousand pages was entered into the grand prize drawings. A total of 168 teens signed up, and they read 135,391 pages. The Teen Advisory Board helped plan the program and suggested prizes, themes, and events. A teen suggested changing to a page-based prize system so the program would be fair to those who read longer books over the summer. The local Friends group provided funds for prizes and donated "bag of books" coupons to be used at one of their book sales. Businesses, including the bookstore and a local pottery painting shop called Artcentric, donated other prizes, and the local skate shop gave Brown a discount when she purchased a skateboard deck for one of the grand prizes.

"Discover New Trails @ your library"

Boise Public Library

Boise, Idaho

Youth Services Librarian Linda Brilz has held summer reading programs for teens at the Boise Public Library for a few years; for the past several years she has offered teens the option of participating either by coming into the library or by entering online. For 2004 she had the library's IT (information technology) department set up a link in several places on the library's website; a general summer reading program page linked to information on the programs for children, teens, and adults with an online registration link, and links were also placed on the children's page as well as the teens' page. Teens simply had to click on the link to get the form and fill in the information. The form included general information about the program (dates, rules, and so on) and spaces for participants to write in the author and title information for two books they had read. There was also a space to write a short review and a box they could check if they were willing to let the library print the review in the teen newsletter. When they hit the Submit button, the information was sent to an email address that Brilz monitored. She printed all online submissions so they could be entered into the prize drawing. She allowed teens to count almost anything as a book: books, books on tape, comics, magazines, even picture books if participants were reading to younger siblings or babysitting charges. Brilz noted that the majority of the entries she received were novels, but she did get the occasional picture book; she said, "Anything to get them to read and/or enjoy books works for me." A total of 237 teens entered the program, and they submitted 1,959 title entries.

Brilz sent a few of the teens' reviews, which were brief and sometimes quite witty. Here are a few of them:

Dreadful Sorry
by Kathryn Reiss

> My reading teachers have always had the two chapter rule. Read two chapters and then if you still don't like it you can stop. This book didn't need that rule. It grips you from the beginning and keeps a strong hold until the very end! Great book!
>
> —Chelsea W.

Your Travel Guide to Civil War America
by Nancy Day

> We all know that in the American Civil War the country split-up into two parts, right? What I didn't know was everything else! This book tells you all you need to know and more! It's a great one!
>
> —Spencer S.

The Scarlet Letter
by Nathaniel Hawthorne

> He uses the word "ignominy" 23 times. Not a very good book.
>
> —Winnie C.

Teens who read at least two books and submitted one form received a free ticket to a Boise Hawks Baseball Club baseball game (a minor league team affiliated with the Chicago Cubs), free entrance tickets to a local rodeo, and a coupon for a free individual-size pizza from the local Round Table Pizza. The Friends group provided funds for a free paperback book for each teen who read at least two books, and for five $50 gift certificates to various places (local mall, bookstore, computer store, music store, and so on) as prizes in the drawing. Brilz said, "This is the most fun—making the calls to tell them they 'won.' It's amazing how many kids are down here (having broken numerous traffic laws, no doubt) within minutes of the phone call. Most of them are more excited about picking a book off the prize cart than anything else." The Hawks, the rodeo, and Round Table Pizza all donated the tickets and coupons given to the teens.

Each year, Brilz uses the theme chosen by the summer reading cooperative the library belongs to, but her Teen Advisory Board (TAB) helps her come up with program ideas and ways to promote the program. The TAB and Brilz thought the 2004 theme was rather bland, so they decided to go with more multicultural programs. Teens also help at the summer reading registration table, signing people up and giving out prizes to those who have finished.

The other programs for teens included a "Middle Eastern Afternoon." One of the library staffers is Iranian, and she came in an Iranian outfit and taught the teens an Iranian dance; an Egyptian woman came in Egyptian clothes and taught the teens to write their names in Arabic and Farsi; and a woman from India did henna tattoos. Twenty-five teens attended, which Brilz said is great for a Friday afternoon. An Egyptian restaurant provided food for the program.

Library staff member in Iranian traditional dress, Boise Public Library

"Discover New Trails"

St. Louis County Library

St. Louis, Missouri

The St. Louis summer reading program for teens was held countywide and was designed to remind them that reading is not just something they do for school but is something they can do for recreation as well. Teens who registered could read whatever they wanted: books, magazines, comic books, graphic novels, newspapers, and so on. At registration they received a sheet that contained three coupons; they needed to read any three items to turn in a coupon, and for every coupon turned in they could select a prize from the mystery box. The coupon was also entered into a number of raffles held at the branch level and systemwide. A total of 3,115 teens registered for the program. The mystery boxes at each branch library included Sonic restaurant coupons (for a free medium slush, a free corn dog, or a free single-topping sundae), FM radio flashlights, stop watch necklaces, Indian print slap bracelets, feather pens, diamond-cut pen key chains, a rock climber key chain with compass, Earth squeeze balls, mini neon gel pens, maze pens, and foot-shaped key chains. Each branch gave away a T-shirt with graphics based on the program theme and a prize pack donated by Sonic that included pens, a beach ball, food coupons, a T-shirt, and a very cool beach blanket that converted to a backpack. The systemwide raffle prize was a mountain bike. Many local businesses sponsored the reading program, including Sonic, the St. Louis Cardinals, and AMF Bowling Lanes.

Libraries in the system offered a variety of programs for teens, such as a Teen Trivia Night, a Karaoke Contest, a Duct Tape workshop, crafts events to design fun stuff to decorate school lockers, the second annual teen computer game contest (with prizes), a babysitting workshop, a painting workshop, a workshop to create a Chinese lantern, a Teen Night when teens could read, play games, and just hang out with their friends, a family Boggle tournament just for fun, a Teen Mystery Theater in which teen actors presented a mystery to be solved, a Library Survivor program in which teens were invited to "explore the library jungle," and a Teen Board Game Night.

Teen Summer Reading Program

West Bend Community Memorial Library

West Bend, Wisconsin

West Bend Community Memorial Library has a teen summer reading program that coincides with the children's summer reading program each year; each program runs for six weeks. The library is part of the National Collaborative Summer Library Program and uses the theme and graphics provided by the consortium. In 2004 Young Adult Librarian Kristin Lade sent letters along with flyers and posters to the middle and high schools in her community. Teens registered and received a reading folder to keep track of the time they spent reading. When they reached twenty hours, they got their name on the wall of fame and got to enter the grand prize drawing, which included prizes valued at about $100 each—a bike, a DVD player, an American Girl Doll, and so on. They could continue to read, and for every three hours of reading, they received a smaller prize. There were food coupons and event passes, and the library had a large treasure box full of prizes for all ages; Lade made sure there were teen-friendly prizes such as temporary tattoos, woven friendship bracelets, and key chains. More than three hundred teens participated; the library system didn't separate the teen reading from the children's reading. In both age-level programs, a total of 1,257 participated and read about 17,000 hours.

Local businesses donated prizes or money to purchase prizes. The library was able to put together bags with assorted items that were used as prizes for weekly trivia and guessing contests, and three Readers of the Week were selected for each age group—preschool, reader (elementary), and YA.

"Get Lost @ your library!"

Ada Community Library

Boise, Idaho

The Ada Community Library's Teen Center advisor, Leslie McCombs, used the theme provided by a summer reading consortium for her library's 2004 teen summer reading program. Teens signed up and received a card with five hours of reading to mark off in half-hour increments. When they completed the card, they turned it in to receive a prize. The library offered prizes for the first three cards completed, and the teens could continue to read to have more entries in the grand prize drawing. Teens who completed the first card received a ticket to REI's climbing wall and a coupon for free fries at Burger King; those who completed the second card received a ticket to a Boise Hawks baseball game and $2 off either bowling or billiards at the Boise State University Student Union Building; and those who completed the third card received a free book. The grand prizes included: a coupon for Café Olé, a $20 gift card for Game World, $10 gift cards at Fred Meyer (a grocery and department store), coupons for in-line skating rentals at Newt and Harolds (a local sports store), and Flying Pie Pizza gift certificates. The main library saw 101 teens come in who read a total of 1,255 hours. McCombs said her Teen Advisory Board helped her with planning for the programs; if they didn't like an idea she proposed, the library wouldn't do it. The Boise Hawks and two local pizza companies sponsored both the children's and teen summer reading programs.

"Teen Treasures" Summer Reading Club

Vigo County Public Library

Terre Haute, Indiana

The Vigo County Public Library (VCPL) used to give teens a choice of counting either hours or books for the Summer Reading Club. This was good for the readers who read long but few books as well as for those who read shorter but many books. The requirements for the teens were less taxing than those for the younger children, on the theory that teens are busier with jobs and activities and that it is more difficult to entice them into the library in the first place. In 2003 the library developed a new concept for its summer reading club—a Family Reading Club. In this club, the library doesn't count the number of books, pages, or time spent reading, nor does it require lists of books or "book reports." The staff created this plan to address the needs of busy families and to promote families working together—and the staff needed a change.

VCPL offered two reading clubs in 2003 and again in 2004. One was a Family Reading Club for all ages. Children could sign up to participate individually or with their family, which was defined as a parent, grandparent, neighbor, day-care group—any type of configuration the children desired. Everyone who participated earned prizes by completing activities on a reading log. The activities included "Read a book," "Listen to an audiobook," "Read a Caldecott Award or Honor Book," "Attend a story time at the library," and so on. An activity was considered to be completed if any one family member who was registered accomplished the task.

Teens going into grades six through twelve could choose to participate in the Family Reading Club, or they could register individually in the Teen Reading Club. The activities to be completed were similar to those for the Family Reading Club but were more teen-oriented. For example, activities included "Read any book," "Read a Michael L. Printz Award or Honor Book," "Read a book based on a fairy tale," "Read a book that is also a movie," "Read a 'Teen Pick' book," "Attend a Teen Program," and "Write a short review of a book for the Teen Book Review Notebook." The members of the Teen Advisory Board helped devise the list of activities for teens and submitted their favorite titles for the Teen Pick bookmark. There were thirty activities in all, with prizes awarded after completion of ten and fifteen activities. The first prize given was a food coupon and a lanyard with a library card wallet. The second prize was a paperback book and an entry to win a family pizza party.

The Reading Club began on June 1 and ran through the Saturday before school started, so everyone had plenty of time to complete activities. Participants filled out a short registration sheet with the names of the family members who were participating, along with a few other details that the library used when putting together statistics about participation. Each club's materials had different graphics and were printed on different-colored paper to help staff members tell them apart at a glance and to help each group feel more "ownership" of their club. About forty teens participated in the "Teen Treasures" Summer Reading Club in 2004, and several others chose to participate with their families in the Family Reading Club.

The Friends of the Library sponsor most of the summer reading club and programs. Other community organizations and local businesses have also helped the library with donations of coupons, prizes for contests and teen programs, and T-shirts for the teens who volunteer at the library. One local radio station has been a sponsor for several years, promoting the summer programs on the air and providing some prizes. A local television station frequently sent a photographer to programs to take pictures that were highlighted on the news. For 2005 Cindy Rider, the School Liaison Program librarian, collaborated with the school corporation in Vigo County to set up a "traveling trophy" for reading club competition between interested schools.

Rider reported that the library's combined theme for 2005 was "Tune In to the Library." Teen Advisory Board members taught Swing Dance moves to other teens, and teens could "tune in to fun" by playing

"Human Monopoly." The game required two partners, one to roll huge dice and handle the money and the other to be the token that moved around a giant board. Teen Advisory Board members created the game board, renaming squares based on books and fairy tales. For instance, "Hogwarts" replaced Boardwalk, and one of the utilities was the "Fountain of Youth." The library also held a food contest and an Ice Cream Sundae contest. Teens made their own ice cream in coffee cans (for directions, see p. 35 earlier in this chapter) and used it to make sundaes. The library provided some basic toppings, and teens brought others from home to share. Finally, teens "tuned in to community service" by making unique, rubber-stamped birthday cards for residents of a local nursing facility.

"Step into Reading . . . Step into Life"
Fresno County Public Library
Fresno, California

Fresno County Public Library calls its summer reading programs Teen Reading Rave, and in 2004 the theme was "Step into Reading . . . Step into Life." The program lasted for six weeks, and each week highlighted a different genre. Posters and bookmarks used shoes as graphics to depict each genre: clown shoes for humor, the dancing shoes of a woman and a man for romance, football cleats for sports, and so on. Several branches displayed their hot picks in shoe boxes and decorated the teen area with shoes. Some teens wanted to trade in their shoes for some of the shoes on display. Teens who registered for the program received a bingo-type game board, with squares for activities including reading time, volunteer hours, program attendance, and book reviews written for the teen website. When they completed the bingo card, they turned it in for a prize and were entered into a branch drawing and a systemwide grand prize drawing. The library didn't keep track of overall reading. About three thousand teens participated in the program. Prizes included tickets to the Fresno Grizzlies baseball games (the local Triple-A team), coupons for a free Round Table personal pizza, and books. Each branch gave away a mini–video camera in the grand prize drawing.

Teens could choose to volunteer at their library for two hours to complete a bingo square; YA Services Coordinator Kelley Worman said that some branches had more than thirty volunteers while others had two. Volunteers assisted with the children's summer program, handled computer sign-ups, and did lots of other general library odd jobs. Some of them became regular volunteers at their branches during the summer.

The library system offered a number of programs for teens during the summer reading program, including spooky storytelling, making coffee-can ice cream (see "Read, White and Blue" earlier in this chapter for directions), duct tape crafts, an edible roller derby (teens used food to build cars judged on best time, best construction, and best appearance), making designer dinnerware, origami, Mehndi tattooing, papermaking, and more.

"Cinema Summer"

Mamie Doud Eisenhower Public Library

Broomfield, Colorado

The Mamie Doud Eisenhower Public Library offered "Cinema Summer" as their teen summer reading program for 2004. According to Gigi Yang, the manager of Young Adult Services, teens entering grades six through twelve could participate in the program and could choose to track their reading by hours or by book. The program had five levels, each requiring three books or six hours to complete. The library also allowed some substitute activities that teens could do instead of some of the reading. They could listen to an audiobook, watch a movie based on a book, fill out a ballot to vote for the Blue Spruce Book Award (the Colorado Teen Book Award), volunteer at the library (ushering at children's programs), or come to a teen program; each activity equaled two hours or one book.

When the teens completed each level, they received prizes. For level one, they received coupons for Muscle Beach Lemonade and for 20 percent off a purchase at Borders Books and Music; for level two, they could choose from various food coupons from local restaurants (smaller-value coupons were combined), including Chipotle, Good Times Burgers, Rubio's Taco, Noodles, Wendy's (a Frosty), Einstein Bagels, Qdoba, Subway, Jamba Juice, or House of Bread (a cinnamon roll); for level three, they received a pass to the Broomfield Recreation Center and a clapboard key chain; for level four, they received a pass to Lakeside, a local amusement park; and for level five, they received a free book.

Teens who finished the program by completing all five levels (fifteen books or thirty hours) got a ticket to enter a drawing for five grand prize baskets. They could also continue to the Director's Cut reading program; they didn't get any more prizes, but they received one drawing ticket for each level completed. The grand prize baskets all had movie genre themes: action, anime, fantasy, comedy, and drama; each contained books and DVDs, popcorn, candy, and coupons for two video rentals. Teens could choose which basket they wanted and put their ticket in the drawing for that basket. The library also held weekly drawings; teens finishing each level filled out a ticket for those drawings. The weekly prize was two AMC movie passes, a Cinema Summer T-shirt, and a free movie poster. The posters came from local video stores and movie theaters. The T-shirts and movie passes were put into popcorn containers, and teens could choose the poster from a bin.

Many local businesses supported the program by either providing funding or donating prizes. A total of 654 teens participated in the program; those who counted books read 2,670 of them, and those who counted hours spent 9,114 hours reading.

"Journeys: Every Book's a Trip!"

South Kingstown Public Library

Peace Dale, Rhode Island

Young Adult Services Librarian Eileen Dyer started the first teen summer reading program at South Kingstown Public Library in 2001; in 2002 the program went statewide. The 2004 program was called "Journeys: Every Book's a Trip!" and it started on July 1. At South Kingstown, 328 teens entering grades six through twelve participated. They could do so on a weekly basis, and each week (and its prizes) was autonomous so they could miss a week (for example, if the family went on vacation) without falling behind. The teens were asked to read for a minimum of thirty minutes a day for five days each week. Each week that they accomplished this, they could stop by one of the three libraries (or Dyer would visit the summer camps or YMCA) and fill out the weekly Journeys form. The completed weekly form was placed into the Journeys box, and the teen received the weekly prize.

Weekly prizes (some were donated by local businesses, some were statewide) included free bowling passes, coupons for a free candy bar at a fine local chocolate shop, coupons for a free large cookie at a local bakery, coupons for $1 off at a local pizza place, coupons for $1 off at a local CD store, discount coupons for a local "way cool" toy shop (Dyer noted that the sixth graders still loved toys), and a "Book Buck" for $1 off on library fines or printing in the South Kingstown libraries. Dyer gathered all the forms from the three library locations and the four camp/YMCA locations and drew for each week's prize.

There were drawings during each of the six weeks, and prizes included food coupons (lots of free pizzas from various shops, sandwiches, hot dogs, burgers, falafel, deli items, ice cream, frozen lemonade); gift certificates from cool local clothing shops; tickets to a place with bumper cars, go-karts, bumper boats, batting cages, and the like; tickets to a local waterslide; coupons to a video rental store; tickets to a roller rink; gift certificates to a bookstore; tickets to the Pawtucket Red Sox baseball games; and three savings bonds (ranging from $50 to $100) from local banks.

The South Kingstown libraries have established a good working relationship with both the South Kingstown Recreation Department and the local YMCA. The librarians meet briefly in the late spring with the coordinators of the summer day camps and arrange a time to stop by each week; they do this for both the children's and teen summer reading programs. Dyer usually makes all the visits to the day camps, three run by the recreation department and one run by the YMCA. The first week she explains the program. Each following week she gives participating readers the Journeys forms, allows them to fill them out, collects them, hands out weekly prizes, hands out any drawing prizes that a teen from that location might have won from the previous week, chats a bit, then goes to the next site. It's a lot of work, but Dyer's efforts mean a lot of teens who might not otherwise have a chance to get to the libraries can still participate in the summer reading program. Dyer also drops off a box of uncataloged, mildly used books at each campsite at the beginning of the summer, so the campers have some reading materials for those occasional rainy days and quiet times. She picks them up at the end of the summer, and she said that if any books are missing, she considers they're in good hands.

Sponsored by the Rhode Island Office of Library and Information Services, the Institute of Museum and Library Services and your local library.

2004 RHODE ISLAND TEEN SUMMER READING PROGRAM

"Get Wired at the Library"

Livingston Parish Library

Livingston, Louisiana

The Livingston Parish Library used the Louisiana state summer reading theme for its 2004 teen summer reading program, reported Youth Services Librarian Stacie Barron. The library is located in a small, rural community, so the state-provided posters, reading logs, and bookmarks helped Barron put together a program for her teens. The program lasted six weeks, and teens who registered were expected to read at least three hours a week for a total of eighteen hours. When they completed the program, they received a certificate, a pair of sunglasses, and a raffle ticket. For each additional five hours the teens read, they received another raffle ticket. At the end of the program, Barron had a drawing with larger prizes: four movie passes to the local theater, a T-shirt, and a book. Thirteen teens participated and read a total of 138 hours.

Barron started a Teen Advisory Board in 2004; the two members helped her by suggesting other programs that the library offered in conjunction with the reading program. An artist came in to talk with teens and draw, and the library had an acting workshop and a poetry workshop. The teens also suggested the types of incentives to give away, and they helped with decorations for the younger children's summer reading program. Barron hoped to expand the group with more teens, but noted that it's difficult to reach them in a rural community.

"New York Is Read, White and Blue"

Rogers Memorial Library

Southampton, New York

Young Adult Librarian Denise DiPaolo used the New York State summer reading program theme and graphics for her young adult summer reading program in 2004, the second year that Rogers Memorial Library had held such a program. DiPaolo asked school librarians about their summer reading requirements, then marketed the program to teens, telling them they could get credit in the summer reading program for reading the books they needed for school.

When teens registered for the six-week program, they received a packet with a list of programs, a suggested reading list, a schedule of events, a pencil, a bookmark, and a reading log. They could read a book and write a short report or book review, do anything library-related, even get "caught" behaving nicely in the library and earn book bucks. Reading a book and writing a report earned twenty book bucks, turning in a review earned ten book bucks, completing a fun library puzzle earned one to five book bucks (depending on the difficulty), listening to an audiobook earned twenty book bucks, and attending a library program earned ten book bucks. DiPaolo handed out random book bucks for good library behavior, for reading to a younger child, for recommending a book, for volunteering to set up or break down for programs, and so on.

DiPaolo used funds from the Friends of the Library and a good library programming budget to purchase small toys and other items from companies such as Rhode Island Novelties and Oriental Trading Company; she also received some coupons from local businesses, such as $1 off a pizza. She kept the prizes behind the desk, and when teens earned one hundred book bucks, they could start spending them on the prizes; "prices" ranged from one book buck to twenty-five book bucks per item, depending on size and value. The library kept a tally for the readers. When teens reached one hundred book bucks, they also received an invitation to the end-of-summer party, with a DJ and pizza. Ninety-five teens signed up, and fifty-five of them completed the goal of earning one hundred book bucks.

DiPaolo set up weekly contests during the summer reading program; each week teens had to answer a question that was based on the program's theme and required a little research. They submitted the completed forms for entry into a drawing. DiPaolo also printed the cover of a YA book with the author's name blotted out and asked teens to identify the author. In 2004 the weekly drawing prize was a DVD. The 2005 theme was music-related, so DiPaolo devised music-related contest questions and offered music CDs as the weekly prizes.

The library offers teen programming every day except Thursday and Sunday: Mondays are games days, Tuesdays are crafts days, Wednesdays are Surprise Days, Fridays are movie days, and on Saturdays the library schedules outside performers. Programs have included juggling workshops, balloon workshops, learning card tricks, a paint and sew craft event, computer workshops teaching teens how to make greeting cards and gift labels, speakers from local museums on such topics as forensic archeology, and chess. In 2003 the library held a Poetry Slam, and in 2004 it offered Book Bingo where teens played to win books (everybody won).

Teen Summer Reading Club

Patchogue-Medford Library

Patchogue, New York

In the 2004 Summer Reading Club, teens registered to participate by filling out a Registration Card that was kept in a large file box. The cards were organized by week and recorded the number of books read, the number of pages read (or minutes listened), the prizes handed out—both weekly and point levels—and the librarian's initials. Teens read books, then completed a Book Reporting Card for each book, recording the title, author, and number of pages (or minutes for audiobooks). They were also asked to write down what part they liked best and why, and their favorite characters or, for nonfiction books, the subject.

Teens could receive weekly prizes for reporting on at least one book. They also accumulated points— 1 point for every fifty pages read or one hundred minutes heard—and received prizes at certain levels: 5 points, 10 points, 20 points, 30 points, and 50 points. Prizes ranged from feather and fish pens (from Oriental Trading Company) to yo-yos, lanyards, decks of cards, marbles, paperback books, blank books/journals, puzzles, squirt frogs, and other fun stuff from Rhode Island Novelty Company and other mail-order places. The 50-point prize was their choice of a music CD. About 175 teens joined the Summer Reading Club and a total of 1,248 books were read.

High school seniors and college students volunteered to help keep records, distribute prizes, and listen to reviews during the program. Young Adult Services Librarian Martha Mikkleson said the library continued its regular programs throughout the summer, including game night, movies, and crafts, and some of the teens participated in the Suffolk County Battle of the Books program.

Mikkleson said she noticed some "cheating" by some teens to get to the 50-point level to get the music CD. For 2005 the library gave out weekly prizes but kept the identity of the prizes secret until the week they were given out. Also, instead of the point levels, the library gave out raffle tickets for every fifty pages or one hundred minutes; there were several prizes in the raffle. Mikkleson also gave out "Librarian's Choice" awards to those teens who participated in teen book discussion groups and other library activities. Mikkleson said that changing the club rules slightly each year helps her staff iron out the kinks and try new things, keeping the club interesting.

"Make It Fly!"

Middle Country Public Library

Centereach, New York

Middle Country Public Library's teen summer reading club for 2004 was called "Make It Fly!" in honor of the centennial anniversary of aviation, reported Laura Panter, Adult and Young Adult librarian. Teens could read anything they wanted, whether it was a book, graphic novel, or magazine. They received a reading log when they signed up, with six numbered tickets. There were six levels to complete, and every time teens read for a minimum of two hours, they handed in the appropriate level ticket to receive a prize until they completed the reading log. When they completed all six levels, they received a Techno backpack. The librarians kept all the tickets that were turned in, and at the end of the club, the tickets were put into the drawing for raffle prizes at the end-of-summer dance.

Sixty-five teens participated in the summer reading club. The incentives for completing the six levels included airplane penlights, stopwatch bracelets, airplane bubble necklaces, temporary tattoos, and lanyards. The Teen librarians (the Teen Team) planned and selected incentives to match the theme, which were all purchased by the library. The Teen Advisory Council assisted in planning the end-of-summer dance, choosing the theme, the decorations, party favors, and music.

The library gave teens opportunities to volunteer as Book Buddies during the summer and offered about twenty-five programs during the season. On Friday nights there were drop-in programs, including a game night, a craft program, poetry and music coffeehouses, and a drama improv class. On Wednesday nights the library had its Anime Club, Share a Book, and Teen Advisory Council meetings. On other nights of the week, or on Saturdays, the library offered computer instruction classes, various arts and crafts events,

health and exercise programs, cooking, dance, a Battle of the Bands, Teen Flicks (teens voted on the movies they'd like the library to show), and more.

The theme for 2005 was Music, and the library offered such music-themed prizes as mood pencils with music quotes, CD pencil sharpeners, mini headset radios, silicone bracelets with music words, and rock necklaces with music notations.

Make It Fly!

2004 Teen Summer Reading Program

"Discover! Explore! Read!"

Herrick District Library

Holland, Michigan

For the 2004 young adult summer reading program at Herrick District Library, the teens asked Young Adult Services Librarian Mary Robinson to choose a theme that related to but remained separate from the Lewis and Clark theme chosen by the collaborative the library belongs to. For the teens, the library ran a bingo-type game, with four different bingo sheets. Teens registered and received the first bingo sheet. After they marked off five items to get a bingo, they received a prize for completing the sheet and were given the next bingo sheet.

On each bingo sheet, teens could read five books or use the center square—"Attend a Library Program"—to substitute for one book. Each bingo sheet included various genres and included magazines, graphic novels (listed as "comics"), books made into movies, and several squares titled "Your Choice." Teens were also asked to list the books they read on the back of the bingo sheet and to rank each book on a 5-point scale, with 5 meaning "Awesome!" and 1 meaning "Waste of a tree!"

For completing the first bingo, teens received a carabiner key chain, and for successive bingos they received a small Earth ball, a paperback book of their choice, and a CD case. A total of 596 teens signed up; 265 completed the first bingo sheet, 174 completed the second bingo, 126 completed the third, and 67 completed the last sheet.

The library's Teen Advisory Board helped with the planning of the summer reading program, including the theme. For 2005 the Teen Advisory Board decided to follow the statewide theme, Joust Read: Join the Reading Round Table.

Discover! Explore! Read!
Teen Summer Reading #1

B I N G O

Magazine	Your Choice	Realistic Fiction	Sports Or Outdoor Adventure	Book Made Into a Movie
Your Choice	Historical Fiction	Non-Fiction	Your Choice	Comics Or Humorous
Realistic Fiction	Your Choice	Attend a Library Program	Mystery Or Adventure	Fantasy Or Science Fiction
Your Choice	Non-Fiction	Historical Fiction	Realistic Fiction	Your Choice
Comics Or Humorous	Fantasy Or Science Fiction	Sports Or Outdoor Adventure	Biography	Your Choice

➤ Read books from the categories listed on the bingo card.
➤ Record book titles and authors on the back.
➤ Score, horizontally, vertically or diagonally.
➤ When you have a bingo, return your chart to the Young Adult or Children's desk and pick up your key chain. Last day to pick up prizes is August 28.
➤ Ready to read more, then, pick up a yellow bingo card.

Herrick District Library

READING LOG

Name _____ Phone _____

List the books you have read.
Rate each book by circling a number.
5 = Awesome!   3 = OK   1 = Waste of a tree!

Title _____

Author_____

Rank   5   4   3   2   1

Title _____

Author_____

Rank   5   4   3   2   1

Title _____

Author_____

Rank   5   4   3   2   1

Title _____

Author_____

Rank   5   4   3   2   1

Title _____

Author_____

Rank   5   4   3   2   1

Look for the TEEN PICKS book display
to find the favorite summer reads of other teens.

Young Adult Services
Herrick District Library & Herrick North Side Branch

Herrick District Library

SPECIAL PROGRAMS

In addition to running summer reading programs for young adults, many libraries offer a wide variety of other programs, ranging from craft workshops to mystery nights, Fear Factor–type programs, anime and other movie showings, and much more. These kinds of programs are fun, entertaining, and educational and help to make the library more of a community resource. Some librarians made an effort to tie their programs in with books, while other connections were more subtle. The common thread among all the programs is the librarians' desire to provide more services to their young adults. Some programs are described briefly in the preceding chapter on reading incentive programs, and here are some other highlights.

CULTURAL EVENTS

Benicia Public Library in Benicia, California, had a Hawaiian Luau in 2004. A local hula teacher and some of her students performed some hula and then tried to teach some of the teens. Teen Services Librarian Kate Brown reported that watching the boys learning to hula was especially hilarious. There was a Hula Hoop competition, and everyone ate "Hawaiian" food—aloha chicken, macaroni salad, taro chips (like potato chips but made from taro root), *malasadas* (the Portuguese version of beignets), and *haupia* (coconut pudding). Brown's husband, who is from Hawaii, made the *haupia* from scratch.

The summer reading program at the Amesbury Public Library in Amesbury, Massachusetts, had a multicultural theme. Norma Chang from New York City gave a Chinese cooking lesson to teens. The program was limited to fifteen teens and was filled to capacity. The teens had a great time learning about the different ingredients that made up some of their favorite Chinese dishes. They were able to cook their own dish under Chang's watchful guidance, using electric woks.

A teen led a program called "Hair by Holly," in which twenty teens learned how to do cornrow braids. Each girl braided the next girl's hair and so on, until everyone had cornrows.

Twenty-six teens at the Peabody Institute Library in Peabody, Massachusetts, explored Indian culture at a two-hour-long program called Taste of India. They sampled Indian cuisine cooked by Young Adult Librarian Melissa Rauseo, watched the movie *Bend It Like Beckham*, and had henna tattoos done by a professional henna artist. The tattoos were a big hit. The library asked all the teens to have permission slips signed by their parents, and many of the parents thought it was such a cool program that they wanted tattoos also. This was one of the most popular programs ever offered by the library, according to Rauseo.

INFORMATIONAL EVENTS

Carmel Clay Public Library in Carmel, Indiana, offered an informational program for teens called "Facts of Flight: Navigate the World of Aviation." The pilot who presented the program, Dave Newill, is the husband of one of the children's librarians. He is a licensed pilot and a former military pilot, and he asked the library if he could put this program together. He brought a short video of the Blue Angels (the U.S. Navy precision aviation team based at Naval Air Station Pensacola, Florida) as well as aviation maps of Indiana and gave everyone who attended a poster showing a cockpit instrument panel. All the posters were donated by the local airport he uses, which also sent brochures on flying lessons. Newill went over the basic principles of flight and navigation and answered any questions the teens had. Using the posters, he described the different gauges on the instrument panel and explained how to read an aviation map. The teens who attended already knew quite a lot about flight and asked lots of technical questions. Using Styrofoam egg cartons, Newill taught everyone how to make models of gliders that another Indiana man designs and flies. Newill also brought a model airplane to show everyone how the different parts of an airplane move. Autumn Gonzales was the librarian in charge; seven teens attended and really enjoyed the program.

The Mastics-Moriches-Shirley Community Library in Shirley, New York, offers a lot of programs, but even Librarian Mary Maggio was doubtful about the program proposed by a former librarian named Tara. An avid horse lover and owner, Tara contacted Maggio in 2004 about a program she had developed to teach teens about horses. In a one-hour program, she taught the teens about tack, riding, and horse care. Maggio wasn't sure it would be very popular, so she asked Tara to add a riding component to the program. She arranged for the teens to take a trail ride at a local park that has a stable and gives lessons. Twenty teens registered for the program, which was held at the library on a Friday night. Then they all met Tara the following Monday morning at the park for the trail ride. The staff at the stable divided the group in half and took each group on a half-hour ride. The stable took care of any insurance concerns and provided helmets to all the teens.

FUN AND GAMES

Benicia Public Library in Benicia, California, held a Wacky Olympics competition. The games included Nerf archery, Hula Hoops, DDR (Dance Dance Revolution), and musical chairs. The library also had karaoke, which they have every year. The room was decorated with flags from countries around the world, and the library served treats from different countries.

The summer reading program at Natrona County Public Library in Casper, Wyoming, is sponsored by the Casper Rockies, a minor league baseball team. On June 29, 2004, the Rockies invited teens to come to a picnic and a tour of their ballpark before watching the team take on the Idaho Falls Chukars. Because the Greater Casper Summer Reading Program for teens was called "Get Lost @ your library," the Rockies called their program and game "Get Lost, Chukars."

Young Adult Librarian Melissa Rauseo of the Peabody Institute Library in Peabody, Massachusetts, offered teens an Online Sleuths mystery program. She adapted one of the mysteries from *The Mysteries of Internet Research* by Sharron Cohen and created a website with the crime and information about the suspects. Teens had to determine who was telling the truth and who was lying. The person who lied was guilty. Any young adult who submitted the correct solution to the crime was entered into a drawing to win a $50 gift certificate.

The Robert Cormier Center for Young Adults at Leominster Public Library in Leominster, Massachusetts, is nicknamed "The Bob." In 2004 Young Adult Services Coordinator Diane Sanabria held a Cranium Tournament for teens in grades seven through twelve. She divided participants into four teams of four teens each. They played by the rules of the game, which is advertised as "the game for your whole brain." They took a break for snacks in the middle (the tournament lasted from 2:30 to 5:00 p.m.). Each teen on the winning team received a $10 gift card to Barnes and Noble (paid for by the Friends of Leominster Library); Sanabria purchased six cards, so she did a door prize/raffle with the remaining teams to give away the extra cards. She ran a second Cranium Tournament later in 2004, with three teams of five teens each. For that tournament, she put the snacks out on the tables so the teens could munch as they played. For the second tournament, she also purchased $10 gift cards to Barnes and Noble to give to the winning team members and to raffle off to the other teams. She held an "Apples to Apples" tournament in 2005.

The Allen County Public Library in Fort Wayne, Indiana, has held a chess tournament for teens since 1999. It's an unrated tournament, played just for fun, but it has always attracted some strong young chess players as well as those who are just beginning to play the game. One of the Young Adult specialists in the library system is a chess enthusiast, and he has been emceeing the tournaments for several years; a family of chess players has volunteered to score the tournament since the first year. One of the YA librarians at the main library coordinates the registration, obtains the trophies, arranges for the food and drink, and handles all other housekeeping details to run the tournament. In 2004, 110 teens registered, and 80 actually showed up to play. Because the main library has been undergoing massive reconstruction since 2002, the tournament was held at the First Wayne Street United Methodist Church, less than a block from the library's temporary location. Because the library purchases very nice-looking trophies and provides lunch and snacks, this program tends to be expensive. It cost roughly $700 in 2004, with the additional cost of rental for the church space. The library's summer programs are supported by a local foundation. Young Adults' Services Assistant Manager Ian McKinney said that, because of the steady increase in interest in the chess tournament, YAS added a Chess Club, which meets twice a month all year long. Many families in Fort Wayne homeschool their children, and many of them like the Chess Club and tournaments. Children's Services has also held annual summer chess tournaments for children in kindergarten through fifth grade, which leads them right into the YA tournaments as they hit sixth grade.

The Orange County Library System in Orlando, Florida, offered a Toga Party to kick off its first teen summer reading program in 2004. Teen Program Specialist Danielle King and her Teen Voices volunteer group designed the event as a sneak peek at what was going to happen at the library over the summer for teens. Teen Voices developed challenges and games based on the idea that in the ancient Olympics, athletes competed not only in physical activities but also in tests of bravery, endurance, and intelligence. The activities included a mini Wacky Olympics with obstacle courses, a bravery test based on *Fear Factor*, a mind test using Greek mythology, and an endurance test using Forbidden Words. A costume contest and the crowning of Zeus and Athena followed the challenges. The library was decorated with columns, gold gossamer draperies, gold balloons, golden apples, and ivy leaves. The teens ate Greek food such as hummus (chickpea and sesame paste dip) with pita bread, Greek salad, Nectar punch (the drink of the gods), and baklava.

The Wilmot Branch of Tucson-Pima Public Library in Tucson, Arizona, has offered teen mystery nights as an after-hours program for several years. In 2004 twenty-five teens participated. They met in the library's meeting room where the crime for the night was described (the library has used murder, attempted murder, theft of a library book, and other crimes). The teens worked as detectives as they traveled to locations within the library to examine evidence, compare fingerprints, and research information related to the case. Suspects, played by volunteers or library staff members, had been identified earlier, and they presented their alibis to the teen detectives. The teens could work alone or in teams. Eventually, they reconvened in the meeting room after their investigation, and they revealed the suspect that they believed to be guilty. The library then served refreshments.

The Bettendorf Public Library in Bettendorf, Iowa, offered a Library Survivor scavenger hunt in 2004. Young Adult Librarian Maria Levetzow described it in her publicity materials: "You're stranded on a deserted island. How will you survive? Oh, wait, no . . . it's a deserted library!" The after-hours program was designed as a team event, but individuals could sign up and be assigned to a team. Twenty teens attended the program. Levetzow reported that she used a program designed by Rosemary Honnold, but she apparently didn't adapt it enough or have enough staff to help the teens move along with the hunt. The program was scheduled for one and a half hours, but none of the teams was done by then. While Levetzow thought it was a disaster, the teens had a great time.

Allen Park Public Library in Allen Park, Michigan, just a few miles south of Detroit, ended the 2004 summer reading program with a Lock-In for all participants who earned at least 1,200 points during the program. Young Adult Librarian Karen M. Smith filled the five-hour, after-hours Lock-In with activities for the teens. The evening started with a pizza dinner and awards ceremony. Then, professional storyteller Yvonne Healy took over with her ActUp! Workshop. She led the teens through some physical activities. In one, each participant had to choose someone to be his or her "enemy." Participants were not to let anyone else know who their enemy was. Then they had to walk around the room, always making sure to stay as far away as possible from their enemy. Because no one knew who was whose enemy, the teens ended up running in circles. Smith described the scene as hysterical. The other activity was a version of "Whose Line Is It Anyway?" where the teens acted out certain situations. In one of them, one person got to be the Queen, and the other participants were in charge of making her laugh. Whoever won got to marry her. When the workshop was over, the scavenger hunt began. The teens formed groups, and each group was given a list of trivia questions. The answers to the questions were written on the backs of certain books in the library. Using the clues given, the teens had to find the book and write the answer for the correct question. When they were done answering all fifty questions, they turned in their answer sheet and returned to the meeting room. The team that was the fastest and had the most correct answers won, and they received books as prizes. The evening ended at 11:00 p.m.

At the San Diego County (California) Library's Spring Valley Branch, YA Librarian Denise Stutzman conducted a Teen Jeopardy game in 2004 that attracted competitive boys. She created a Jeopardy board and wrote the questions and answers in a grid. She posted the categories (such as Movies, History, Animals, World, Books, and more) on the wall, and under each category she taped a piece of paper with a number value on it. A contestant could choose "History for $400," and the paper with 400 would be taken down. Stutzman read the question, and teens called out their names in lieu of a buzzer. An assistant kept score as the teens tried to rack up points.

The Fresno County Public Library in Fresno, California, offered its Fearful Food Challenge program in 2004. Young adults competed individually or in teams for four rounds in which they had to eat gross concoctions, like hot mustard sardines over sauerkraut or four kinds of baby food mixed together (everything was totally edible). Participants had to provide permis-

sion forms and releases signed by their parents. During the course of the program, a couple of the teens threw up, which they didn't seem to mind, and of course the audience loved it.

The Fresno County Public Library also offered a program where teens could meet George the Giant, who was one of the consultants for the *Fear Factor* television show that inspired so many Food Fear Factor programs in 2004. George the Giant is an expert in sideshow stunts; he walks on glass, hammers a nail into his head, puts a balloon into his nose and partially out from his mouth and then blows it up, and lies on a bed of nails—and these are just some of his stunts. He did all these things at the library, and he talked about the history of sideshows.

The Upland Public Library in Southern California offered a mystery program for teens in 2004. Children's Services Library Assistant Randee Bybee had the library purchase a mystery program through Upstart, and the Teen LAB (Library Advisory Board) created the props and scenery and hosted the program. Bybee said it's one of her favorite programs, because the teens basically run it. Preparation started with the design of the crime scene about ten weeks prior to the program; the teens drew the design and used it to plan everything. They filmed the suspects so it appeared they were being interviewed by a news team. On the day of the program, which lasted two hours, each group of eight teens was considered a detective team. They selected someone to be their head detective and spokesperson; Bybee said this approach works best and creates a fun atmosphere for the teens to work together. While the detective teams went over their findings after viewing the crime scene and the police desk, the library served pizza. The teens devoured the pizza, and as they handed in their deduction sheets, the LAB director assigned priority numbers to them. After each team had turned in its sheet, the director and his two assistants went over them in priority order, and the first sheet to have all the correct deductions won. The winning team received movie tickets, mystery books, and journals, and there were other miscellaneous items for the runners-up.

Villa Park Public Library in Villa Park, Illinois, offered a trivia contest based on *A Series of Unfortunate Events*. There were three levels (easy, medium/moderate, and advanced), each with its own two-sided trivia sheet of twenty multiple-choice questions. Participants could complete any or all of the levels and were free to consult the books and take the sheet(s) home to work on. The contest ran for four days, at the end of which the completed trivia sheets were reviewed to determine which ones had the greatest number of correct answers. Winners were notified by telephone and received a Snicket-themed prize (such as a book or toy). Although there weren't a great number of participants, those who did participate were very enthusiastic and worked fervently on the trivia questions.

Danbury Library in Danbury, Connecticut, held a Harry Potter Trivia Contest, which the library's teen volunteers put together; they came up with the questions themselves. They opened the contest to grades six through nine. The teens helped decorate the program room to look like the Great Hall at Hogwarts (including "floating" candles) and set up four long tables (for each "house"). Some of the teens dressed as the teachers at Hogwarts. Teens who came were sorted into the houses, and each house competed as a team. Orange drink, jelly bellies (to represent Bertie Bott's Beans, which were beyond the library's budget), and gumdrops were served to the contestants as they answered the many (and difficult) questions. Each member of the winning table received a large Hershey candy bar, then everyone participated in a raffle for other prizes.

The Northbrook Public Library in Northbrook, Illinois, held a joke contest to go along with its "LOL (Laugh Out Loud)" teen summer reading program in 2004. Youth Services Librarian and Teen Specialist Karen Cruze said it started as a drawing that asked teens to write down a favorite joke. Despite the instructions, about half the jokes were mildly offensive, so she took those out. She then asked her fellow Youth Services staff members to help her choose the ten best from the remaining jokes, and of those ten she chose her favorite joke as the winner. As Cruze said, "Not entirely what I had in mind originally, but it worked out okay. When you have to, bunt."

CRAFTS

Teens at Upper Arlington Public Library in Upper Arlington, Ohio, came out in droves for the annual Red, White, and Blue Tie Dye program that is held annually just prior to July 4. They brought shirts, bandanas, socks, and other clothing items to tie-dye and wear on the Fourth. Young Adult librarian Betty

Sheridan said that more than one hundred teens participated in 2004. She always holds this program outdoors and has teens work together in groups at big tubs; she said it's fairly easy to do because there are only two colors to work with. All participants get rubber gloves so they won't get dye all over their hands, and the library supplies them with care instructions and plastic grocery bags to carry their dyed items home. Adults cut the rubber bands off items, and teens work at the plastic dye tubs. Some teens also help participants rubber-band their items. Sheridan said that as of 2004 the program had never been rained out; the program can move indoors, but it's better outside with so many people at the dye tubs.

The Bettendorf Public Library in Bettendorf, Iowa, had a program called Fairie-ality; Young Adult Librarian Maria Levetzow used the book *Fairie-ality: The Fashion Collection from the House of Ellwand* written by Genie Shields to design the program. Levetzow had volunteers and staff—even her mother—drying and pressing flowers all summer. The only real expense was a few dollars for a pound of silica gel to dry the flowers. On the day of the program, fifteen teen girls, younger sisters, and moms used the book as inspiration to create their own fairy fashions using the dried and pressed flowers. Levetzow reported, "You've never seen such a quiet group of teen girls. It was almost eerie. But it was a terrific craft, it was book-related, and it encouraged creativity. What more could a library ask?"

Some branches of the Montgomery County Public Libraries in Maryland offered a Claytime workshop for teens. Potters from Glen Echo Pottery brought their pottery wheel to the library and demonstrated how to make a bowl on the wheel. Then those teens who were interested could try their own hand at making a bowl for themselves. People were more than willing to get dirty in order to get a chance to use the pottery wheel. They could take their projects home, and they could use self-hardening clay and paints to make another item. The program was advertised for ages ten and up, but most participants were preteens and teens.

YA Services Coordinator Kelley Worman at the Fresno County Public Library in Fresno, California, reported on a craft program that didn't go according to plan. The library had advertised a "Crazy Pens and Cool Binders" craft activity, where teens could make some cool stuff for back to school. They were going to make pens wrapped in colorful Fimo Clay. The instructions called for the pen inserts (stick pens) to be wrapped in Fimo Clay and baked in the oven. The librarians used toaster ovens, but the pen insert melted and caught fire. They had to eliminate the pen project and just have the teens decorate their binders.

The Vigo County Public Library in Terre Haute, Indiana, offers a "Combo Craft" program every summer. In 2004 School Liaison Program Librarian Cindy Rider combined sand art with glass painting to create candleholders or room decorations. Staff members and friends donated empty Frappuccino, salad dressing, and other bottles for the program. Rider demonstrated a few basic techniques of sand art using household items such as spoons, pickle forks, and skewers and then showed the teens how to prepare the glass by applying a light coating of rubbing alcohol to the glass surface with cotton balls and then letting it dry. It just takes a few minutes, but it helps the craft paint adhere to the glass. In addition to colored sand, the library provided other materials such as aquarium gravel, small shells, and beads for layering in the bottles.

The Gail Borden Public Library in Elgin, Illinois, offered a number of summer programs for teens. One of the more popular programs in 2004 was the aromatherapy craft program. It was so popular that the library had to schedule a second session. Twelve teens came to each session, for a total of twenty-four. They made two bars of scented glycerin soap, their own lip balm, and a small jar of milk bath. Library staff melted the beeswax for the lip balm and the glycerin cubes for the soap, using a microwave oven, so teens wouldn't have to handle hot ingredients. The teens then added their choice of coloring and scent and used their creativity to give their soaps a layered look. Each teen also decorated the outside of a baby food jar that was then filled with homemade milk bath. The supplies for the program were easily obtained at the local Hobby Lobby store and the grocery store. Staff members donated the baby food jars. Youth Services Librarian Lisel Ulaszek and other staff members used Joe Rhatigan's book *Soapmaking: 50 Fun and Fabulous Soaps to Melt and Pour* and Jennifer Traig's *Beauty: Things to Make and Do* for instructions on how to make the lip balm, glycerin soaps, and milk bath. The teens had a wonderful time and so did the librarians. The only downsides to this program were that the librarians couldn't fit more than a dozen teens in the kitchen at a time, and it took a while for the glycerin and beeswax to melt and both materials hardened quickly, so the

teens had to be patient while they waited to receive their ingredients. The supplies, especially the lip balm containers, the glycerin, and the dyes and scents, really added up in cost; the total cost of the program was probably about $250 for the supplies, so this was a fairly expensive program to do for a small group of teens. However, Ulaszek thought it was well worth it.

In 2004 the Upland Public Library in Upland, California, offered a sewing craft program that appealed to both boys and girls—Butt Pillows! These pillows are made from old pairs of jeans. The participants brought an old pair of jeans that they no longer wanted or needed (or had outgrown). The first thing they did was cut off the legs of the jeans; then they sewed the leg openings closed with colorful embroidery floss, using a simple whip or over stitch. After they sewed up the leg openings, they decorated the front and back of the jeans with various donated, scrounged, and purchased items, including patches, buttons, trim, silk flowers, studs, beads, old jewelry, and more. The library provided all the materials for the teens to use. Once they added their decorations to the jeans, they stuffed them with pillow batting and sewed the waistline shut with the embroidery floss, using the same stitch. The library allowed two hours for the program, but many of the perfectionists went home with a plastic bag full of pillow batting to finish their pillows at home.

In 2004 the Villa Park Public Library in Villa Park, Illinois, ran a few programs based on themes and ideas from Lemony Snicket's *A Series of Unfortunate Events*. Jean Jansen, the assistant head of Youth Services, created an Invention Contest. Participants (in grades five through twelve) could come in any time during the week of the contest and pick up a kit that consisted of a sheet of directions and a bag containing an assortment of several (five or six) items (contents varied from bag to bag). All the items in the bags were purchased at American Science and Surplus, a local store. They sell all manner of odds and ends, surplus and remainder items, and many little medical, scientific, and mechanical parts and items [editor's note: it's a hoot to read the item descriptions in the catalog]. Jansen bought a large variety of items and sorted them into the bags for the participants. Each person received a randomly selected bag, along with the instructions to create a device that the character Violet Baudelaire could use in any of the *Series of Unfortunate Events* books, which participants could name and explain if they wanted to. The single rule was that participants could only add their own tape, paper clips, or rubber bands to their bag of items to create their inventions. At the end of the week, all entries were due, and Jansen and another Youth Services department member privately reviewed and judged all the entries. Jansen said this was a difficult task, because all the entries were very thoughtful and creative and included written descriptions. They finally decided on the three most innovative and well-done inventions and awarded Snicket-themed prizes to the winners. However, they decided to put all the entries on display in one of the library's large display cases. It took until fall to secure all the permissions from the participants and their parents/guardians, but they were able to have the display up during the back-to-school season.

Henna tattooing, or Mehndi, was another popular program that was offered by a number of libraries all around the country in 2004. Ada Community Library in Boise, Idaho, was fortunate to have an artist who had recently emigrated from India who did all the tattooing work on the teens who attended. Any teen who wanted a henna tattoo had to bring a permission slip signed by a parent in order to get a tattoo. The library provided games and other activities for the teens who were waiting for their turn. Some had the tattoos done on their hands, some on their arms, and a few on their legs. Many of the teens loved showing off their tattoos for the librarian's camera.

Henna arm tattoo, Ada Community Library

STAGE AND SCREEN

In 2004 to tie in with their "Cinema Summer" teen summer reading program theme, the Mamie Doud Eisenhower Public Library in Broomfield, Colorado, offered several hands-on programs involving movies.

For the program on Character Makeup, the library invited Denver-based Greg Reinke, who owns a makeup and special effects company, to do the workshop. Reinke also runs a huge haunted house every Halloween, but he usually does his work in Hollywood. He talked to the teens about his background and how he got started in the business. He picked a volunteer from the group and transformed her into a monkey with a spiky green wig. He showed all the steps of how to attach a prosthetic and the makeup to cover it and blend it into the person's facial features. After that demo, he put out makeup kits and helped the teens make their own ghastly wounds. He showed them how to create bruises, burns, fractured bones, broken noses, and lots of blood. Teens worked on each other or on themselves.

Two film school students, Philip Armstrong and Zack Milan, helped Gigi Yang, the library's manager of Young Adult Services, with a Stop Motion Animation workshop. Yang collected lots of McDonald's toys and bought bendable toys and other small figures from thrift stores. She borrowed digital cameras and video cameras from the city's IT department and asked teens to bring in their own digital and video cameras, if they had them. Armstrong and Milan divided the teens into

Henna designs, Ada Community Library

groups of five. Armstrong started the workshop by giving an overview of the general principles involved in stop-motion animation and the roles the teens could play in developing their own film. Teens then could choose a role in their own group: director, lighting, filming, and two "actors" who moved the figures. They then selected the toys and props they wanted to use from the stash Yang had brought and wrote a rough outline of their story. Each team had a three-fold backdrop, and Yang provided markers and papers for the teens to decorate it. The teams worked for about two hours, filming. As they finished, Yang, Armstrong, and Milan downloaded the digital films to a laptop and threw them into Windows Movie Maker. The teens also had a beginning and an ending screen to write their title and credits so each film would have a similar look. Then they hooked everything up to an LCD projector and everyone watched the finished works. The films that teens did on video cameras were hooked directly up to a television set. They also showed parts of *Wallace and Gromit* and Nick Park's early works so the teens could see how he started out and so Armstrong and Milan had time to clean up and compile the teens' work so they could show it.

Armstrong and Milan also worked with Yang on a Video Production workshop. Milan wrote five generic scripts that could be interpreted in a number of ways. This program was held in the Broomfield Auditorium, which is attached to the library. The teens were split up into groups of five or six and they chose their roles: director, lighting, sound, filming, and actors. Armstrong gave an overview of filming techniques, illustrating different shots and angles to use in order to capture what they wanted to show. Each group was then given a script and worked to create their own story based on how they were going to light and film it. The library provided some sound effects that they could use, and Yang brought in random props such as flowers, telephones, hats, and so on. The auditorium's technician gave the teens a tour of the space and showed them how to use the light and sound board. Each group had a five- to ten-minute run-through and then immediately filmed their story on the stage. The other groups watched while they waited for their turn. When each group was done, everyone watched all the films on a television. The library burned the stop-action animation and video clips onto CDs that the teens could keep. Yang said that she really enjoyed the creativity of the teens, the hands-on aspect of the

workshops, and the immediately viewable results. She thought the teens would have been willing to work much longer on each program.

The Gail Borden Public Library in Elgin, Illinois, held a program on Stage Combat in 2004; twenty-five through thirty teens entering grades seven through ten, both girls and boys, attended. A local theater in the Chicago area called Metropolis Performing Arts Centre does many six-to-eight-week summer programs for kids. Youth Services Librarian Lisel Ulaszek asked the centre's education director if some instructors would come to the library to present a program for 90–120 minutes. Ulaszek decided that stage combat was an element of theater that many teens probably hadn't seen. Two trained theater professionals came out. They started with an explanation of stage combat (all the physical acts the audience sees onstage, such as hair pulling, face slapping, and so on). They then demonstrated each technique step-by-step and took the teens through the techniques, remaining mindful of safety throughout. The teens learned several techniques, including how to safely do a convincing hair pull and a face slap and how to convincingly fall to the ground as if they fainted or were knocked out onstage. The teens had a great time, and the cost to the library was minimal, only $5 per teen. Ulaszek said she would definitely work with this theater again and do another theater-themed program for a summer workshop as it proved to be very popular.

The Ada Community Library in Boise, Idaho, provided an opportunity for some of the teens to write and perform a play. The teens, including a number of homeschooled students, met at the library and worked on the play for three months, writing it, planning it, creating costumes and props, and rehearsing it. They called their original work *Snow White and the Seven Disasters*. All their work culminated in a performance at the library before an audience of friends and family members (more than fifty came to watch the play), and it was incredibly rewarding for the teens.

BOOKS

Upper Arlington Public Library in Upper Arlington, Ohio, held a Book Jam and Pizza day at the beginning of summer. Young Adult Librarian Betty Sheridan brought books, and teens came prepared to discuss their favorite books. Sheridan said this program

Snow White and the Seven Disasters cast members, Ada Community Library

allowed her to get an idea of what the teens were reading on their own, and it helped keep the book dialogue going. Pizza was, of course, a big hit. This is an annual program, and sometimes Sheridan has a "best pizza contest" along with the book discussion. As she put it, "Food—Books—Teens—what could be better?"

FOOD

The South Kingstown Public Library in Peace Dale, Rhode Island, has held a Make Your Own Sundae Party every year for more than four years to kick off the Teen Summer Reading Program. All young adults who are entering sixth grade and up can attend and make their own ice-cream sundae and also sign up for the Teen Summer Reading Program, which in 2004 was "Journeys: Every Book's a Trip!" Young Adult Services Librarian Eileen Dyer said that a local supermarket and the Friends of the Library donate funds so she can buy "gallons and gallons" of ice cream, assorted toppings, candy toppings, and whipped cream. Her Teen Board of Advisors (TBA) helps with the event, and they hold it on the front lawn of the main library, which makes it a great promotion for the library as well. Although they restrict sundae makers to those at least entering sixth grade, they do let some younger

kids indulge in some melty bits at the end of the program. Every year about seventy-five to eighty young adults attend the kickoff.

Natrona County Public Library in Casper, Wyoming, held a Pizza Taste-Off in 2004. Teens were invited to a blind pizza taste test at the library. Six local stores (Domino's, Papa John's, Daddy O's, Godfather's, Pizza Hut, and Papa Murphy's) all donated cheese and pepperoni pizzas. Library staff removed the pizzas from the boxes, cut the pizzas into small pieces, and numbered the pieces for the taste test. Teens then worked through six of each type, voting on the best cheese pizza, best pepperoni pizza, best crust, best sauce, and best overall pizza. They recorded their votes on ballots, which were quickly counted to determine the winners. After the tasting, the teens made ice-cream sundaes and hung out with their friends. Some teens got a little sick from all the pizza and ice cream, but the teens encouraged the library to hold another taste-off. The local paper covered the event, and pictures appeared in the paper. Young Adult Specialist Emily Daly decided not to give out the results of the taste-off.

The Southfield Public Library in Southfield, Michigan, held a cooking program for teens as part of its "Get the Arts in Your Smarts" summer reading program. Youth Teen Services Librarian Shari Fesko happened to start chatting with a young woman who owned a catering business and lived near the library, and Fesko mentioned she wanted to do a cooking program; the young woman offered to assist. Fesko gave Tanya, the young woman, money for supplies that she purchased and brought to the library. It was a high-maintenance program, but Tanya was a great sport and the teens loved it. Tanya showed them how to properly coat chicken wings and gave them a container and directions on how to cook them at home. She also showed the teens how to make a cold pasta salad in a baggie. Teens filled their baggies with cooked pasta, vegetables of their choice, cheese, and a favorite dressing, then they shook the bags to mix everything together. They could take their salad home to eat with their chicken wings. Tanya talked a lot about food safety and healthy eating as well. Fesko expressed surprised at how many boys attended and enjoyed the program. She said this was a program worth repeating, although she and Tanya would try to find something easier to prepare than chicken wings the next time.

The Peabody Institute Library in Peabody, Massachusetts, also held a Pizza Taste-Off in 2004, along with its Fun 'n Games Day. The afternoon began with the teens playing typical party games, all of which were described at http://www.partygamecentral.com/. Winners of each of the games got to choose a wrapped prize. Once they unwrapped the prize, they were allowed to switch prizes with other people. After the games were finished, the pizza taste-off began. Five local pizza places each donated two large, uncut cheese pizzas. The twenty-two teens who attended were able to sample each of the five pizzas without knowing its origins. They then voted for best crust, best cheese, best sauce, and best all around. While the teens ate the rest of the pizza, the library staff tallied the votes and announced the winners. The library sent thank-you notes to each pizza place and certificates to all the winners. Young Adult Librarian Melissa Rauseo reported that the program was a big hit and the teens wanted to see it become an annual event. She said she got the idea for the Taste-Off from Rosemary Honnold's book *101+ Teen Programs That Work*. She also declined to tell which pizza place won what categories.

Every summer, Vigo County Public Library in Terre Haute, Indiana, offers a food contest for teens going into grades six through twelve, planned by the Teen Advisory Board. In 2004 the food contest was "Name That Pizza!" The library provided pita bread (for the crust), pepperoni, cooked hamburger, sausage,

and bacon; the teens could bring other items from home (M&Ms, anchovies, mushrooms, gummy worms, marshmallows, and so on). The teens created their own exotic personal pizzas using various ingredients, then named their pizzas, writing the names on labels attached to toothpicks. Members of the Teen Advisory Board baked the pizzas and then "judged" them by creating a unique category for each entry, so that all participants were winners. The winning categories were printed on die-cut doorknob hangers and placed by each plate. Categories included "Best Use of Marshmallows" and "Fishiest." While the pizzas were baked and judged, the professionals from Chicago's Pizza put on a demonstration of "dough throwing" and gave the teens (and the librarian!) a chance to try their hand at it. Then it was time to look at all the pizzas and eat them, of course! Chicago's Pizza donated all the cheese and pizza sauce for the contest.

Teen Program Specialist Danielle King of the Orange County Library System in Orlando, Florida, reported that one of the most popular programs that took place in the summer of 2004 was the "Fear Factor" event. All the challenges in this program were inspired by events in scary novels. Fifteen teens entered to compete in the hair-raising challenges, while more than thirty teens watched. The teens had to eat Bug Blood Soup (crushed strawberries, honey, raisins, and bread) just like Darren in *Cirque du Freak* by Darren Shan; Cow Brain (chicken dumplings mixed with corn syrup and red food coloring) as in *Hannibal*

"Name That Pizza!" contest entries, Vigo County Public Library

by Thomas Harris; and Chocolate Covered Bugs (chocolate-covered Rice Krispies) like the people in *Man Eating Bugs* by Peter Menzel. They also competed in noneating games like the Cockroach Hunt (a timed competition to see how many plastic cockroaches teens could find with their toes in a pool of wood shavings, apple juice, and Tootsie Rolls), symbolizing the place where Matt from *The House of Scorpions* by Nancy Farmer had to live in filth; Eyeball Tossing (bull's-eye played with sticky eyeballs thrown onto a clown's face), symbolizing the creepy clown in Stephen King's novel *It*; and Lost (finding the way out of a room while blindfolded and dealing with strange noises, odors, and flying objects), symbolizing the feeling the characters experienced when they were lost in the novel *Buried Alive* by Gloria Skurzynski. The overall winner earned a huge candy bar and a free book. The program was so popular that teens asked for another, which King designed for 2005.

Fear Factor was a popular program theme in 2004. The North Liberty Community Library in North Liberty, Iowa, also had a Food Fear Factor program that attracted thirty teen participants. Assistant Director/ Teen Librarian Jennifer Garner said that she was surprised at how many teens lasted through most of the challenges and that she had to do some nasty stuff to eliminate most of them and get a winner. She had promised that if no one made it all the way through, she would eat one of everything—she was glad she didn't have to do that. She had three rules: (1) they had to chew, (2) they had to swallow, and (3) they had to show her their empty mouths. The food items included Pimples (cherry tomatoes filled with cream cheese and chives) that had to be squeezed into their mouths; Baby poop (baby spinach lasagna)—they had to eat a teaspoonful each; Whole baby oysters (canned)—if any teens were allergic, they had to eat SpaghettiOs mixed with chocolate syrup and whipped cream; Clam milk shake (ice cream, milk, and minced clams); Dried meal worms (three flavors); and Chocolate-covered ants and crickets. Garner timed the drinking of the milk shakes and had the top six fastest finishers go on. When they had all finished the whole thing, Garner blended all the leftover foods, including the SpaghettiOs mix, into one gloppy, hideous, gray-green mixture that reeked. A number of the teens gagged, and the local cable department that taped the whole program made a hilarious DVD. Garner again timed the teens drinking a paper cup (three ounces) full of the horrible stuff. Only two managed to drink the entire cupful. One girl managed to drink the whole thing in less than a minute—and without gagging! Garner said that girl must have an iron stomach. The prize was a basket with "good" (i.e., junk) food such as candy and microwave popcorn, and also soda, a cup, and movie passes.

The Montgomery County Public Libraries in Maryland offered a program that allowed teens to taste chocolates from around the world, hear music, see new books, and meet other teens. The library staff decorated the room with witty sayings they found on a website, and they set up displays of books about chocolate, new YA titles, and new DVDs and videos with teen appeal. Different types of chocolate were broken up into small pieces and several flavors were featured, such as white chocolate, bittersweet, and orange. As a DJ played CDs and chatted with teens, people could walk around, taste the chocolates, and fill out a form saying which chocolate they liked best and why.

ART

The Southfield Public Library in Southfield, Michigan, offered a two-part drawing/cartooning program with a local artist who had just graduated from the Center for Creative Studies. Imran, the artist, was an amazingly talented man who really clicked with the teens who attended. Before the program, he presented Youth Teen Services Librarian Shari Fesko with a list of "real drawing supplies" she had never heard of, but she was able to purchase them at a local art store. This was a popular program that attracted teens, and Fesko mourns that Imran moved out of the country to pursue his goals.

The Nashville (Tennessee) Public Library holds a summer reading logo contest for teens every year. In 2004 teens were asked to design a logo for the theme "Retro Reads." The contest was open to teens aged twelve to eighteen who have Nashville Public Library cards. Each teen could submit one entry, done in black and white in pen or other black-and-white medium, on 8 1/2-by-11-inch paper. All entries had to be camera-ready and had to include the words "Retro Reads" in the design. All entries were forwarded to the Young Adult Committee of the library system (it has twenty-two locations), which voted on the winning logo. The winner was then submitted to the Public Relations department, which used the logo on all summer reading program promotional items, including the T-shirts that were given away in the program. The winner received a $50 gift certificate to a local art store. Teen Anna Thomsen was the 2004 winner.

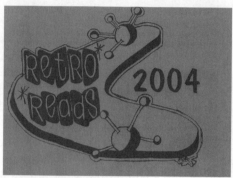

Nashville Public Library

The North Liberty Community Library in North Liberty, Iowa, held a photo contest for the first time in 2004. The theme was "Making Waves," and for the contest, teens were to take photographs, have them developed, and bring them to the library. The library provided poster boards, stickers, and other decorations so the teens could make a collage portraying the concept "Making Waves" using their photos. Eight teens participated, working on their collages during free

time at other library programs. The public access cable channel staff judged the entries based on specific criteria established by the library; they did a fabulous job and provided feedback sheets to every contestant. The winner received a digital camera.

The Montgomery County Library in Maryland held a teen summer reading poster contest in 2004, and the winning design was used for the cover of the library's annual *Teen2Teen* booklet and for publicity items such as bookmarks. The library advertised the contest in all the branch libraries, with posted signs and flyers. Poster contest committee chair Barbara Shansby sent out press releases to several local newspapers and sent a copy of the press release with a short letter to all the high school art department chairpersons, asking them to publicize the contest and to require participation for their students. The library's website also featured information about the contest. When all the entries were submitted, the YA librarians met to choose finalists; they tried to choose designs they thought would appeal to teens and were artistically superior. Shansby met with a group of fifteen teens, all high school age, who had been doing volunteer projects for the county. She explained the purpose of the poster contest and asked them to choose, by silent ballot, the design they thought would do the best job of advertising the teen summer reading program. It took a couple of rounds of balloting before the teens chose the winning design.

Photography contest

1. Take a disposable camera.
2. Take photos of anything to do with making waves (water, controversial subject, you can stretch the meaning of "making waves" however you like).
3. You are responsible for developing your photos by July 13.
4. You will have opportunity to mount between 2–8 photos on poster board for display at the July 13 program and throughout that week in the library anytime we are open—DO NOT INCLUDE YOUR NAME ON THE FRONT OF POSTER BOARD.
5. Finish by July 16 and submit for contest.
6. There will be 3 impartial judges for the photos.
7. Blue Ribbon Prize: digital camera. Second place will receive a small prize as well.

North Liberty Community Library

MUSIC

The Mastics-Moriches-Shirley Community Library in Shirley, New York, offered a program called "Extreme Mixing and Spinning," designed to give each teen participant the chance to experience what it would be like to be a DJ. The library owns a great sound system with all the equipment that a DJ needs, and they hired Sal, a professional DJ, to run the class. He taught the teens how to mix the music, work the board, "scratch," and do all kinds of DJ things. Each teen got ample time to use the equipment and experiment while getting tips from Sal.

The Bettendorf Public Library in Bettendorf, Iowa, started off its summer with a Teen Street Dance, which ran from 7:00 to 10:00 p.m. on a Saturday night.

A professional DJ played music, and sixty teens came and danced, ate, and danced some more. Local pizza place Happy Joe's sold pizza by the slice, and the library gave out Blue Bunny ice cream. Door prizes were also given out. The teens asked for the program, but Young Adult Librarian Maria Levetzow said it was expensive because of the fee for the DJ. She was willing to do it again, though, if she could figure out a way to cut down costs.

The Montgomery County (Maryland) Public Libraries set up a series of teen band concerts over a five-week period during the summer of 2004. Two bands played outdoors each Thursday night, from 7:00 to 9:00 p.m. The library worked with the Montgomery County Department of Recreation and with the Montgomery County Police Department, the former to help set up and provide sound equipment if needed, and the latter to provide security. The library requested audition tapes from bands that had members between thirteen and nineteen years old. The Department of Recreation had held a Battle of the Bands earlier in the spring and gave the library the names of the top bands from the competition; the library contacted music teachers in the middle and high schools and put an article in the local community paper asking for bands to audition. A small teen advisory group of mostly middle school students helped the library staff listen to the audition tapes and choose the bands that would play. The music was heavily rock, punk, and emo, with some reggae and elements of jazz. The Department of Recreation even sent an ice-cream truck to some of the concerts, and at each concert they held a drawing for two tickets to a nearby theme park.

The Elizabeth Public Library in Elizabeth, New Jersey, collaborates with a community after-school/summer program called SOAR (Special Opportunity for Achievement and Reawakening). Elizabeth's Office of Youth and the New Jersey Department of Health and Human Services manage the program. SOAR provides free tutoring, physical fitness opportunities, and other extracurricular activities for children aged six through fourteen; there are hundreds of kids in the program, and the leaders are always looking for new activities. In 2004 the library staff thought a partnership with SOAR would be a good match. They decided to do an Elizabeth Idol program, based loosely on the *American Idol* television program. It turned out the SOAR kids were the brave ones willing to go onstage and sing in front of an audience of other SOAR kids and teens from the library. Kimberly Paone, the supervisor of Adult/Teen Services, said that her library teens preferred to work behind the scenes. They served as judges, set up the stage, and sat in the audience. The program was successful and was repeated in 2005, with a karaoke machine so kids wouldn't have to sing a cappella. Paone said that, because one of the real *American Idol* finalists in the 2005 season was an Elizabeth music teacher, Anwar Robinson, the concept of Elizabeth Idol will remain popular for some time.

The Middle Country Public Library in Centereach, New York, held its first Battle of the Bands with twelve high school garage bands playing over the span of four hours. At least four hundred teens showed up to see the Battle, which was sponsored by several local radio stations and local judges in the music industry. That was the largest teen audience the library has ever had for any event.

HEALTH AND BEAUTY

The Mastics-Moriches-Shirley Community Library in Shirley, New York, has a working relationship with a beauty consultant who has been presenting hair, nail, and makeup programs for several years. For the 2004 reading program's "Extreme" theme, Librarian Mary Maggio wanted something a little different, and she and Lori, the consultant, decided to give the girls who attended a makeup makeover. The girls were asked to bring their makeup to the library one Friday night, and Lori brought some as well. She evaluated each girl's current look and gave tips on how to make a complete change, asking each what she was looking for. Lori then got each girl started, and they finished the work while she went on to the next girl. Each girl left looking and feeling "fabulous," and the library gave each of them a little bag of makeup.

VOLUNTEERS AND
TEEN PARTICIPATION IN LIBRARIES

The first edition of *Sizzling Summer Reading Programs for Young Adults* described how a few libraries had started Teen Advisory Boards (TABs) and other similar groups, and how some libraries had instituted various volunteer opportunities for the teens they served. In the years since 1998, the number of Teen Advisory Boards has grown dramatically, and even small, rural libraries now have them. Still more libraries have provided volunteer work for teens as part of their summer reading programs. Some have gone beyond having teens work on basic library tasks such as shelving; some libraries have programs for teens to work with younger children as reading buddies, while others provide opportunities for teens to do programming with the children. Some of these activities were described in the summer reading programs chapter earlier in this book, but here are some additional activities and programs.

TEEN ADVISORY BOARDS

At Vigo County Public Library in Terre Haute, Indiana, the Teen Advisory Board meets once a month throughout the year. The members discuss the library's plans for the Teen Reading Club and Family Reading Club and give their opinions regarding such things as format, rules, artwork, and content of the clubs. They also suggest programs that will interest teens and help to plan and carry out the programs.

The Bettendorf Public Library in Bettendorf, Iowa, has a TAB that meets monthly from January through April, and active members are then invited to a TAB party in May, the Saturday before the summer reading program begins. Membership in the TAB has been averaging around twelve to fifteen, and most are girls. The teens choose the special events the library's Young Adult Services will offer during the coming summer, help to plan them, decorate the library, and do other things as needed. They also cosponsor the library's literary anthology, the *Scribe*. Every year, three TAB members choose the works to be included in the *Scribe*. The group serves refreshments for the library's author reception during National Library Week. Members also help at book sales for the Friends of the Library, at fund raisers for the Library Fund, and anywhere else the library needs them.

Allen County Public Library in Fort Wayne, Indiana, has had an active Teen Advisory Board for several years. The teens come from all over the county, and meeting places alternate between the main library and one of the branches from month to month. The TAB has participated in the pilot program for YALSA's Teens' Top Ten project, and the members help with programming and planning for the summer reading program. For the public-service announcement to advertise the Young Adult Summer Reading Program, TAB members write the script and perform, and the local public access cable station, located in the main library, tapes the announcement. The PSA is shown on the public access channels as well as the local broadcast television channels during the late spring and the early weeks of the summer reading program.

The Teen Advisory Board at Northbrook Public Library in Northbrook, Illinois, started in 2003. There were about twenty-five members in the spring of 2005, with sixteen to twenty showing up for any given meeting. The TAB meets for an hour every other month during the school year. The members are in sixth through twelfth grades, with about half in middle school and half in high school, and the members attend six different area schools; about one-third of them are boys. The Youth Services librarian and Teen specialist, Karen Cruze, said the demographics couldn't be any better. The Young Adult area serves grades six through twelve and comes under the umbrella of the Youth Services department. In 2004 Cruze surveyed TAB members for their input in planning the summer reading program. They helped her decide on decorations for the department, and they suggested linking the smiley faces for the LOL theme with the emoticons they used in their emails and text messages.

Carmel Clay Public Library in Carmel, Indiana, has a Teen Library Council (TLC) that works with Young Adult Services Manager Hope Baugh. Membership in the TLC is limited to twenty-five teens in seventh through twelfth grades; prospective members must complete a written application and an interview. The teens commit themselves to meeting every month to discuss what everyone has been reading/watching/listening to, to give their input on library issues related to teens, and to help plan programs for teens, including the Young Adult Summer Reading Program. They help Baugh to come up with the theme and structure of the program, based on their own ideas and on written evaluations from teens who participated in the previous summer's program. The TLC goes on two book-buying trips each year to help select books for the YA collection. In 2004 there were thirty-seven TLC members who volunteered a total of 583.75 hours of their time to the library.

Rogers Memorial Library in Southampton, New York, has a Teen Advisory Group (TAG) that meets every other month. Usually there are eight and sometimes ten teens at each meeting, which are pretty informal, according to Young Adult Librarian Denise DiPaolo. For the summer reading program, the TAG chooses the movies for the Friday night showings and suggests other programming ideas. They also help to unpack the boxes of new books—DiPaolo gives them the first chance to reserve the new YA books. They help to decorate the YA area for the summer reading program, they set up "favorite book" displays, and they suggest improvements and changes to the library.

A Teen Advisory Board helps the Washington Public Library in Washington, Missouri, with planning various activities and programs, including the summer reading program. There were thirteen members of the TAB in 2004; they met once a month during the school year, and sometimes twice a month if they were working on a program or project. The members also helped with the children's summer reading program by serving snow cones at the kickoff, among other activities.

TEEN VOLUNTEERS

In addition to the work done by members of the Teen Advisory Board, Vigo County Public Library in Terre Haute, Indiana, provides regular volunteer opportunities for around fifty teens each summer. These teens work at the main library and at the branches, and they assist with the Family and Teen Reading clubs by recording the reading reported by participants and by distributing prizes. They also assist with programs, children's story times, and special projects, such as preparing craft materials for workshops. The library holds a special recognition party for the teen volunteers at the end of the summer.

The West Bend Community Memorial Library in West Bend, Wisconsin, actively recruits summer teen volunteers. Youth Services Librarian Kristin Lade sends out postcards to teens before the summer, letting them know the date for the volunteer orientation. Lade said she likes the experienced volunteers to come to orientation and help the new teens understand how things work; sometimes they even remind her of things she forgets to mention. The volunteers run the summer reading program, and at orientation Lade reviews the upcoming program, explains their duties and the rules, hands out parent permission slips (which must be signed and returned before a teen can volunteer), and creates the summer schedule. The teens also make ice-cream sundaes. Two weeks later, they get together on a Saturday and tie-dye T-shirts, then write their name and "SRP volunteer" on their colorful new shirts. The teens choose how many hours they want to work each week, and they are responsible for showing up on time and working and for finding a replacement when they can't come in. Lade lets them know that if they can't come in on a particular day, they at least should call her and let her know. The library has an SRP booth set up where children and teens come in with their reading folder and get prizes for their hours spent reading. The booth is manned during certain hours, and if it's slow, the volunteers can shelve videos or paperbacks, organize the reading folders that have been turned in, stock prizes, prepare craft materials, or read a book.

At North Liberty Community Library in North Liberty, Iowa, Assistant Director/Teen Librarian Jennifer Garner has a Teen Advisory Group that helps her with programming at the library. In addition, teens help with the children's program, acting as group leaders for the children. On "program day," about a dozen or so teens stay all day (working 9:00 a.m. to 5:00 p.m. or later) and provide help of all kinds.

The Bettendorf Public Library in Bettendorf, Iowa, has a summer volunteer program that is run by the head of Youth Services, Tami Chumbley, and the volunteer coordinator, Caran Johnson. They hold an introductory meeting and sign up teens who wish to help with various events for younger children. For example, the library usually offers a make it/take it craft day for young children, and the teens help with that. Chumbley and Johnson also tell the teens about the Tech Teens program that Young Adult Librarian Maria Levetzow runs; this volunteer program trains teens to help library patrons one-on-one with the computers.

The Tucson-Pima Public Library in Tucson, Arizona, depends on teen volunteers to help run the children's summer reading program. The library recruits between 150 and 200 teen volunteers during the summer months. They work in all the branches of the library, explaining the reading program to the children, awarding incentives along the way, and encouraging them to keep reading.

The Orange County Library System in Orlando, Florida, developed the Teen Library Corps (TLC) during the summer of 2004 to inspire teens to give back a little "TLC" to their library and community. Teens aged thirteen to eighteen were encouraged to join, and during the first summer and fall, thirty-seven teen volunteers completed more than 450 hours of community service. By spring 2005 the TLC had forty-five members and had completed even more hours of community service. There are three distinct volunteer programs within the TLC: Teen Voices, Program Aide, and Techno Teens. Teen Voices was the first program developed, in September 2003, and was the library's first attempt to reach out to the commu-

nity's teens. It's a teen advisory board that meets once a month to plan programs, make suggestions about teen services, and discuss teen issues at the library. There are between ten and twenty active members, with a president, vice president, and secretary. The library also rewards special efforts by the teens, such as special projects and milestones in individual community service hours completed. Photographs of the teens who receive these awards appear on the IT website described later in this section.

Orange County Library System

The Program Aide program was developed in the summer of 2004 and became the most popular program for teens at the library. This program allows teens to volunteer in the children's and teen departments of the library on a weekly basis. The teens perform a variety of tasks, ranging from assisting with programs to clerical work. Because of the aide program, the library has a more active teen community. Many of the teens who volunteer have the opportunity to meet other teens from around the county. Consequently, the teens use the library as their meeting point and attend more teen programs.

Techno Teens is a new addition to the TLC. This group started in January 2005. The members meet once a month to write book, movie, and music reviews as well as to offer advice on how to improve the "IT" (Informed Teens) website run by the library (http:// www.ocls.info/Children/Teen/default.asp). The website provides information on all the teen programming offered by the library, plus information on all the volunteer opportunities and more.

The Allen County Public Library (ACPL) in Fort Wayne, Indiana, has actively recruited summer teen volunteers for several years. The volunteer services coordinator accompanies some of the Young Adult librarians and specialists when they visit schools to promote the summer reading program; in addition to doing a few book talks herself, she talks about the various volunteer opportunities and explains why volunteering can be good for teens. The main library's Young Adults' Services (YAS) and some of the branches have teen volunteers who help with the different programs in the libraries. YAS Manager Mari Hardacre offered a couple of crafts programs led by teens in the summer of 2005.

Teens volunteer at the library all year round, not just during the summer months. Many schools in the community demand community service of their middle and high school students, some as many as ten hours per semester. These teens often work at various tasks in the libraries, such as shelving, doing minor repairs to magazines and books, and so on.

ACPL started a new teen volunteer program in 2004, Team Read, in partnership with Children's Services. This six-week series paired teen volunteers with children in the early primary grades. Teens underwent an interview and a training session, and then they were paired one-on-one with children. Each teen/child pair worked together for the six weeks of the program. The teens read to the children and were active listeners as the children read aloud to them, and they played literacy-building games in small groups. Sixteen teen/child pairs participated during 2004, and the program was repeated in 2005.

The Ridgefield Library in Ridgefield, Connecticut, recruits teen volunteers to help run the children's summer reading program. In 2004, 189 volunteers worked, and Teen Services Librarian Geri Diorio estimated that about 90 percent of them were teens; among other tasks, they listened to the children talk about the books they read. All the volunteers at the library worked about 960 hours during the summer.

The Northbrook Public Library in Northbrook, Illinois, ran its teen volunteer program for the summer of 2004. Twenty teens volunteered and worked between two to six hours a week at specific times. Their main job was to monitor the reading club visits of other teens. They had their own desk in the Young Adult area, and they marked off visits on the teens' sign-up cards, stamped their reading logs, and handed out prizes. Karen Cruze, the Youth Services librarian and Teen specialist, noticed that they did get a little bored at the desk because she had scheduled them to work generally during the slow times. To relieve the boredom, she had them help her update the display of funny books, sort contest entries for the kids' club, and do a lot of copying, cutting, and collating. She fine-tuned the volunteer program and offered it again during the summer of 2005.

Youth Services Librarian Karen DeAngelo at the Town of Ballston Community Library in Burnt Hills, New York, runs two teen volunteer programs each summer: VolunTeen and Book Buddies. VolunTeens must be at least entering sixth grade and can be as old as nineteen; DeAngelo says that most of them are middle school students, but now that the program has run for several years, she's seeing an increase in high school students. When she recruits teens for the program, she emphasizes that their volunteer time counts for community service requirements for Boy Scouts, Girl Scouts, honor societies, and any other group that requires volunteer time and that they can put this on their college applications and résumés. She also tells them that hardworking, dedicated volunteers who come to work on time may ask her to be a reference for job and college applications. She asks them to work two to four hours a week, but she's willing to negotiate hours with really good, independent workers who may want or need more hours.

DeAngelo is the only Youth Services librarian, so the teens have to work when she's at the library. She tries to limit the teens to four at a time, and the two-hour shifts are 10:00 a.m.–12:00 noon, 1:00–3:00 p.m., 3:00–5:00 p.m., and 6:00–8:00 p.m., Monday through Thursday, and all but the 6:00–8:00 p.m. shift on Friday. The teens help with craft preparations, hand out book bucks to younger children, and run the "store," where kids make their choices and buy their prizes (this task alone can keep two teens busy).

DeAngelo runs a weekly take-and-make craft event, and the teens help to trace and cut out the materials for the bags that the children take home. Older teens put all the data from the sign-up sheets on spreadsheets. There are also the standard tasks of straightening shelves, cleaning and sorting puzzles and toys, and so on. DeAngelo also allows the teen volunteers to read; in fact, she insists that all her VolunTeens and Book Buddies join the teen summer reading program. In 2004 she had fifty-four VolunTeens and Book Buddies, who worked 574 hours.

Teens in sixth through twelfth grades can also participate in the Book Buddies program, even if they're in the VolunTeens. DeAngelo says all she does is match the teens to the children, and they make their own "dates" with the children. The library takes names of all children and teens interested in having or being a Book Buddy and notes whether they prefer a boy or girl buddy and whether the teens would be willing to have more than one buddy if necessary. Then DeAngelo matches the buddies on a spreadsheet and informs all the participants of the name and phone number of their buddy. It is then the participants' responsibility to set up half an hour each week to meet in the library and read together. Younger buddies are usually in preschool through third grade, but DeAngelo is flexible, so if a mother says her ten-year-old reluctant reader needs a teen partner to read with, DeAngelo will find an older teen as a match. Book Buddies runs for six weeks, during the summer reading program.

The Kodak Branch of the Sevier County Public Library System in Sevierville, Tennessee, offered teens the opportunity to lead a story time for preschool and young children on a Saturday morning during the summer. Seven teen girls volunteered to do this, and they chose to do a puppet show. They used the picture book *Bubba the Cowboy Prince: A Fractured Texas Tale* by Helen Ketteman; the story is loosely based on the Cinderella tale, with a cow fairy godmother, and Bubba, the hero, is the stepson of a wicked rancher. They put the story into a play format and used hand puppets, a puppet stage, and headgear to portray each character and act out the story as the play was read aloud to the attendees. The teens received community service hours that they were able to use for high school.

The Carmel Clay Public Library in Carmel, Indiana, runs a Teen Volunteer Corps (TVC) during the summer. It is open to anyone going into sixth through twelfth grades and is coordinated by YA Librarian Jamie Beckman. She accepts applications at any time and maintains a large mailing list of more than one hundred names. Once a teen has filled out the TVC application, he or she will be on the mailing list for Beckman's monthly letter of volunteer opportunities. She gathers requests for help from all departments of the library, and she maintains a list of teens willing to be "on call" for sudden requests.

Teens may volunteer as much or as little as they like, depending on what the library needs. Sign-up for most jobs is first come, first served. TVC members help with children's programs, adult programs, and of course YA programs. They also help dust the shelves, recase CDs and DVDs, weed the library grounds, fold and bundle fliers, and more. During the summer reading program, TVC members apply to fill approximately forty-eight Summer Desk Assistant positions. Those who are selected as assistants attend a special orientation and commit to helping to staff the YA desk in two-hour shifts throughout the summer. They help register people, hand out prizes, record books read, and so on. In 2004 the TVC had 150 members who volunteered a total of 1,974.5 hours of their time to the library.

The Indianapolis–Marion County Public Library in Indianapolis, Indiana, holds a special summer program for teens called Reading Giants. The teens who register for the program are either Regular Reading Giants (in grades nine through twelve) or Junior Reading Giants (in grades six through eight). They work as reading buddies for younger children for a certain number of hours, and the library rewards them with a U.S. Savings Bond.

Teens can register at any of the twenty-four branches in the library system, and they are directed to a PowerPoint tutorial on the library's website for training. Each applicant then completes a questionnaire that serves as a test and is checked by staff members at the branch where the teen took the tutorial. After completing the tutorial and passing the test, the teens are paired with one or more children to whom they read. Junior Reading Giants must complete two hours minimum, and Regular Reading Giants must complete a minimum of four hours of reading aloud to their assigned children. Upon completion of their required time, the teens receive an application to get a savings bond. Sallie Mae and various local banks donate the savings bonds. In 2004 there were 347 Regular Reading Giants and 647 Junior Reading Giants systemwide.

The Boca Raton Public Library in Florida uses teen volunteers to help with the children's summer reading program. The teen volunteers sit at a desk and take care of registering children for the reading program, plus they distribute the weekly prizes. When the children come in to register, they get their picture taken and they hang it in the children's area; they are also given a reading log and a bookmark. Then, each week the children come in, write down a book that they read the past week, and post it by their picture; they then receive a small prize. The teens take the Polaroid pictures, post the photos for the children, and take care of all the work needed at the desk. In 2004 twenty teens helped run the program for the library.

The library has also had volunteer teen face painters for a few years. This came about when the library hired an adult face painter for the Summer Kick-Off Party, which attracts five hundred to seven hundred attendees each year, and the line for face painting was so long that the painter had to stay after the party ended to paint everyone who wanted it done. The library decided to have teens trained to do face painting and have multiple face painters at the parties so the lines wouldn't be so long. In May the library hires a face painter to teach a class of teens how to face paint. She goes over techniques, gives them ideas, discusses do's and don'ts when face painting, and gives them time to practice on each other. Then, the library calls these teens to be the face painters at the Summer Kick-Off and Farewell to Summer parties. The teens enjoy being a part of the party and they enjoy working with the children, who are glad they don't have to spend the whole party standing in line. Teen Coordinator Shilo Perlman usually limits the teens who attend the face painting workshop to twenty. In 2004 twenty teens participated in the workshop, thirteen showed up to work at the Summer Kick-Off Party, and then only four showed up to help at the Farewell to Summer Party.

In 2004 the Danbury Library in Danbury, Connecticut, offered teens the opportunity to become puppeteers in a summerlong program called the "Jester's Puppet Workshop." It tied into the medieval theme of the young adult summer reading program. About fifteen teens came every week for one and a half to two hours and made puppets and rehearsed the story of Peter and the Wolf. They designed their own puppets, using papier-mâché, balloons, and all kinds of materials. Some of the puppets were as large as the puppeteers, who had to wear black when they performed. They used the orchestral music of *Peter and the Wolf*, so they didn't have to memorize any lines. One of the boys wrote and sang a song about the wolf, which none of the adults ever expected. At the end of the program, the teens performed their show for young children and their parents. More than fifty children and parents, including some parents of the teen performers, attended.

The library also offered a Teen to Tot Story Time for the Wednesday walk-in program. Two teen volunteers were assigned to one story time, and they worked together on the theme, props, and so on. They also worked with the Teen and Children's librarians to get approval for their story and any help they needed. They chose the books, finger plays, flannel board stories, poetry, and a craft to do with the children. The librarians gave advice about techniques and about what works and doesn't work for a story time. Librarian Dymphna Harrigan contacted the teens the week before the program to make sure everything was okay,

and she attended the program to take photographs. She did say that librarians who do this should be prepared in case the teens are late arriving for the program, but she didn't have any no-shows. She has worked with various teen teams for this and said that their programs are always good.

Teen Council Volunteers at the library register all summer reading participants, hand out prizes for participants up to sixth grade, and keep records, tracking the number of books read for prizes. The program has places for fifty teen volunteers every summer, and they usually log more than one thousand volunteer hours each summer.

The Middle Country Public Library in Centereach, New York, offers a Book Buddies program in the summer, which pairs teens with children for one-on-one reading sessions. About seventy teens in grades six through twelve volunteered in 2004. The library held three evening sessions per season with two half-hour programs in each session. The teens who came (usually twenty at any given session) were matched with individual children. Children had to be at least three years old. Book Buddies also read to children at other events during the summer.

The Herrick District Library in Holland, Michigan, has had a Teen Volunteer program since 2000. That year sixteen teens gave 299 hours of service during the summer. In 2004 twenty-three teens worked 450.5 hours at Herrick, and six teens worked 186.5 hours at the North Side Branch Library, for a total of 637 hours. Young Adult Services Librarian Mary Robinson reported that the library recruited the teens during May. Volunteers had to be at least twelve years old, and they each pledged to give at least twelve hours of service during the summer. Those who were selected attended one of several training sessions and were given a special T-shirt that they wore when they worked to identify themselves to patrons and staff members.

The volunteers' first job was to prepare the Summer Reading Program packets, which takes at least two nights every year. During the first week of the summer reading program, the teens staffed the registration desk and signed up the children who wanted to join the children's summer reading program. Robinson reported that the library received excellent reports from parents and library staff on the job the teens did during sign-up. The teens then worked all around the library. In Tech Services, one girl relabeled the entire adult biography collection. In AV, several teens shelved materials. In Adult Services, several teens worked shelving periodicals, withdrawing books, and performing other tasks. In the Children's department, two teens were regular shelvers, and others shelved in the YA area. In the office, teens counted and put into rolls the coins that patrons toss into the library's fountain and did some filing. At the North Side Branch, teens shelved AV and children's materials and helped with summer reading sign-up and other programs. One teen worked regularly on the branch's Mad Science Monday programs. A fun project for 2004 was learning to make balloon animals. The library had a table at WOOD TV's Park Party at Kollen Park, and five teens and Robinson made hundreds of balloon animals for the children who attended. The teens also made balloon animals at Herrick's carnival, and other teens helped with other games.

Herrick District Library also has a Puppeteens program every summer. In 2004 six teens participated. The head of Youth Services at the library was a theater major, so she led the group. She also wrote and adapted the stories that the teens performed with hand puppets and other props they designed to be held up on sticks. The teens had five practice sessions and performed twice. One performance was at the Hope College CASA summer program for school-age children. About sixty children attended and enjoyed a question-and-answer session with the teens after the performance. The second performance was at a general children's program, before 125 preschool and early elementary school children. The teens who participated in Puppeteens received volunteer credit for the time they spent rehearsing and performing.

Robinson said that her goals for the teens in the Teen Volunteer program are to have a positive work experience, learn good work skills, and enjoy being in the library. The benefits to the library include completion of necessary work, having a pool of partially trained future employees, and giving the teens a positive view of the library. Feedback from the library's staff on the teens' work has been uniformly positive. The library saw an increase in summer reading program participation, which caused an increase in the volume of materials circulated by the library; the teen volunteers were invaluable in helping the library get those materials back on the shelf quickly. Robinson said, "We would not be able to run our summer programs without these teens."

Flamingnet Book Reviews is not a library program but a nonprofit website developed by Gary Cassel and his son, Seth, where students preview young adult books and write reviews. As Seth put it, "My website is for students between eight and sixteen years old, their parents, grandparents, teachers, and librarians who are looking for books to recommend to or buy for their children, grandchildren, or students." Seth was an eighth grader at the McDonogh School in Owings Mills, Maryland, for the 2004–2005 school year. Gary's hobby is computer programming, while Seth loves to read, and they combined their interests to create Flamingnet. They provide a link on the website for students in middle and high school to send an email if they are interested in reviewing books for the site.

Each student reviewer needs to have an adult sponsor (parent, teacher, or librarian) who will be responsible for making sure that the student completes and submits the book review(s). They can choose new and advance books for review from a list on Flamingnet, and the books are sent to them by mail; the teens have one month to complete the review. In most cases, the students will be able to keep the book that they review. In spring 2005 Flamingnet had twenty student reviewers ranging in age from middle school to college.

A number of publishers send advance reading copies of their books for review, and some authors send books directly to Flamingnet as well. Diane Scharper, a writer, editor, and teacher at Towson University, is a contributing editor to the website, and Bart Raeke is the marketing director.

The Cassels also have summer opportunities for teen volunteers interested in learning about and assisting with the web marketing of Flamingnet, including the production and distribution of an e-newsletter to Flamingnet's membership.

Flamingnet is an associate member of Amazon.com; this means that for every item purchased through the website, Flamingnet receives a small credit ($0.15–$0.25) per item from Amazon. The Cassels use this credit to purchase books for underprivileged young adults and for libraries that don't have money to purchase books for their collection. The ads on Flamingnet may irritate some web visitors, but the income from those ads pays for the costs of running the site. Flamingnet also offers links to places where people can donate old books, and they welcome suggestions of any students or libraries in need that could benefit from a gift of books from Flamingnet.

OUTREACH TO SPECIAL POPULATIONS

In the first *Sizzling Summer Reading Programs for Young Adults*, a number of libraries included descriptions of outreach programs to different kinds of special teen groups, including physically challenged youth, incarcerated teens, rural youth, and others. When YALSA sent out the original survey for this new book, we received very few responses that described outreach programs; therefore, YALSA sent out another request asking specifically for information about summer reading programs conducted for special teen populations. The responses we received were so eloquently written that we are presenting them in the librarians' own voices.

Although librarians would prefer that teens come to the library to participate in programs, some teens either can't get to a library or find it very difficult. In most of the programs described in this chapter, teens have been incarcerated in detention facilities or have been remanded to residential facilities or are homeless; in one case, a Native American university located on a reservation has opened its library to all who live on the reservation. In all the programs described here, librarians or facility staff have adapted public library programs or created their own to encourage reading among the teens in their care.

One library submitted information about its Teen Agency Program (TAP), which has existed since 1996 as a fully funded library outreach program. Allen County Public Library (ACPL) in Fort Wayne, Indiana, has worked since then with six local agencies on a year-round basis, providing reading materials and occasional programs for the teens at drop-in community programs and in correctional facilities. I had the privilege of working with one of the agencies there for five years while I was a YA librarian in the Allen County Public Library's Young Adults' Services department. Ian McKinney, the assistant manager at YAS, said that ACPL currently works with the Allen County Juvenile Center, which is a short-term detention facility for youth awaiting adjudication on their cases; the Allen County Learning Academy, a day reporting school that operates out of Allen County Juvenile Center and serves youth who are under house arrest; the Boys and Girls Club at Fairfield; the Northeast Juvenile Correctional Facility, a state-run, middle-security facility for teen boys aged thirteen through nineteen who have been convicted of crimes and are serving their sentences (this is the agency I worked with); and the Youth Services Center.

In the spring ACPL YAS librarians go to their assigned agencies to promote the summer reading program and to provide pizza snacks or lunches, depending on the facility. For the lockdown facilities, the library provides the reading logs and a supply of prizes that agency staff members use to run the summer reading program in the facility. Agencies are allowed to adapt the program to the needs and rules of their facility; for example, at the Allen County Juvenile Center, any prizes awarded to the teens are held in storage until the teens leave the center. In 2004 two hundred teens in the various TAP agencies participated in the young adult summer reading program.

McKinney said,

> It might be worth noting that (1) completion rate by teens in correctional facilities is much higher than any other population—even homeschoolers. They don't have a lot to do, and so they latch onto what there is to do with great enthusiasm. (2) Teens in correctional facilities are much more likely to have never participated in any kind of Summer Reading experience before. And (3) ACPL's ability to offer the choice of a book at any gift level for these teens is another benefit of our generous grant from the Foellinger Foundation.

Some of the librarians in this chapter mentioned the behavior and enthusiasm for summer reading programs of the teens in various facilities. My summer reading program promotion and pizza party at Northeast Juvenile Correctional Facility was always a highlight of my summer. Whatever crimes they had committed, the boys were still just teen boys, and as I walked around the tables greeting them as they ate their pizza, I received not only thanks for the goodies but also requests for books. I always tried to honor those requests. After the first visit, I learned to keep paper and a pen with me to jot down notes as I talked with the boys. It's YALSA's hope as well as mine that the programs described in this chapter will inspire other YA librarians and specialists to do as much outreach as possible to the different special teen populations in their communities.

Summer Reading for Teen Parents

Public Libraries of Saginaw, Michigan

Our library began an outreach program to teens in the Teen Parent Services program about three years ago (2002). It began with a library orientation program and an invitation to Teen Read Week for a pizza party with a DJ. During the Summer Reading Program, Teen Parent Services becomes an outreach site, and our library staff works with them to make sure that the teens and their babies complete the program. The teens read for twenty hours, and their babies are read to for ten hours. We have a great photograph from 2004 with about sixteen teens and their babies all in Summer Reading Program T-shirts. In 2005 even more teens and babies completed the program.

Teen Parent Services is part of Saginaw County Youth Protection Council, a local United Way agency. The Summer Reading Program is our community-wide SRP for children, teens, and adults, and in 2005 we went with our regional theme "Dragons, Dreams, and Daring Deeds." Children read for ten hours, teens for twenty hours, and adults for twenty-five hours to complete the program. They received a water bottle as an incentive prize halfway through and a T-shirt as an incentive prize for completing the program. The teens who finished were also entered into a drawing for a CD player (there was one prize in each of our five branches).

Here's how the outreach for Teen Parent Services works:

- Our Children's and Teen Services coordinator meets with the Teen Parent Services counselors and others on a regular basis through our community's Birth-Five program.

- In May she makes a special presentation to the teen parents at one of the Teen Parent Services regular programs, talking about reading, the summer programs, and ways to nurture their babies.

- Teen parents and their babies are signed up for the program, and their counselors help them keep track of the time spent reading on their reading records.

- Sometimes reading is incorporated into other Teen Parent Services activities, and it counts toward the Summer Reading Program.

- The teen parents are given a library activity calendar, and sometimes Teen Parent Services provides transportation to the library's children's programs. Sometimes they come on their own.

- We have a program at the library especially for Teen Parent Services clients during the Summer Reading Program. In 2005 we had an activity for the children in one room and took the teen parents into our computer training center to teach them how to use LearnATest, an online database.

- The Children's and Teen Services coordinator and Teen Parent Services counselors distribute the T-shirts at a special program to teen parents who complete the Summer Reading Program. The Teen Parent Services staff really encourage everyone to complete the program, so they have a high completion rate.

We invite the teen parents and their babies to wear their Summer Reading T-shirts at a Teen Services activity. We take a photograph and publish it in our newsletter and/or annual report. We think this program is a great collaboration to encourage at-risk teens to continue their education.

Submitted by Sherrill L. Smith, Assistant to the Director, Public Libraries of Saginaw

Summer Reading for Teens Living on a Reservation

Sinte Gleska University Library

Mission, South Dakota

The Sinte Gleska University Library in Mission, South Dakota, is located on the Rosebud Reservation and is a fully accredited university for the Lakota Nation as well as a public library for the general community. In 2005 the library offered the Summer Reading Program, "Dragons, Dreams, and Daring Deeds," to area children and teens aged two through eighteen from June 13 through August 4. Seventy youth registered, with a total actual attendance of 115 for the program. They were put into age groups: ages two through five, six through eight, nine through eleven, and twelve through eighteen; each group met once a week for one and a half hours.

We made a special book cart with theme-related titles available in the decorated summer reading room, but participants were free to select books from the Youth Section of our library or elsewhere. Children and teens from age six on up had reading goals. During the meetings we made crafts, watched movies, listened to diverse kinds of music, discussed medieval trivia (such as pictures of the actual "ring around the rosie"—the plague), and shared food. On the last day we ate "dragon," which was a giant submarine sandwich creation: the main body was a long loaf stuffed with cold cuts and cheese, the legs were hoagie rolls filled with roast beef, jalapeno pepper spines lined the back, and red pepper strips formed the dragon's fire. It had eyes of hard-boiled egg halves with olives, teeth and claws of almond slivers, and wings of romaine lettuce, and it rested on a bed of lettuce, olives, pickles, and grapes. This year was a goodwill-building exercise, to encourage young patrons to feel at home here and check out books throughout the year.

Submitted by LaDonne Moosman, Youth Services Librarian, Sinte Gleska University Library

Summer Reading for Homeless Teens

Akron-Summit County Public Library

Akron, Ohio

Our Summer Reading Program runs for eight weeks throughout the summer. In 2005 we had three agencies participate in our Summer Reading Program. The agencies were a homeless shelter for parents and children, another shelter with two sites for homeless boys and girls, and an organization serving Hispanic/Latin American families who have moved from various countries to Ohio. Because many of these families and teens are unable to participate at the library, we provide a Summer Reading Box, entry slips, and prizes for each facility site. The Summer Reading Box is the decorated box into which the kids put their entries. After they read their book, they fill out a slip and then drop it in the box. The staff then draw names for prizes every week. In addition to the Summer Reading Box, forms, and prizes, we made a total of nine visits and conducted Summer Reading Programs at the agencies. The programs included cartooning, Library Trivia, pillow making, magnetic poetry, and creating bookmarks. For the teen homeless shelter, we conducted library tours for both the girls' and boys' shelters.

The shelters for the boys and girls had transportation to the library. If the teens had library cards, they were able to use the computers and check out materials. I provided library card registrations to the staff of the shelters so they could have the caseworkers fill them out for the teens. The nice thing that has come out of this outreach is that the group of teens in the shelters have been making visits to the library and using our computers.

For the Hispanic/Latin American families, the volunteer who facilitated the programs checked out items and gave them to the participants for their use. The program attendees spoke English, so we didn't experience a language barrier. The Children's Library has a foreign-language section, but we don't yet have foreign-language materials in the teen area.

I am also going to work with the homeless shelter for families in providing a program (I hope to do monthly programs) for the teen group that meets weekly. I plan to do book talks, crafts, and other literary activities.

We partnered with these agencies through a program called Project Rise. The program is a collaborative relationship between preservice teachers and homeless shelter residents, developed around literacy and service learning activities. The program provides tutors who go into the shelters and assist the kids with homework and with developing life skills throughout the summer and the school year. I just started in my position in June 2005, so my plan is to continue working with this organization on an ongoing basis. I will also attend Project Rise's advisory group meetings. I believe that in the past the library provided Summer Reading Boxes, entry slips, and prizes to the youth shelter, but I am unsure about programming.

I hope to be able to work with all of these organizations in the future. The teens enjoy what we do and the library is another outlet for them. The Akron-Summit County Public Library is interested in doing outreach and meeting the needs of people who cannot easily come to programs in the library buildings. I plan to continue providing outreach and finding ways to provide materials, programs, and information about the library.

Submitted by Heather Ujhaz, Assistant Youth Services Coordinator, Akron-Summit County Public Library

Summer Reading Initiative @ The Parmadale School: "Reading Is the Ticket"

Cuyahoga County Public Library, Parma Regional Library

Parma, Ohio

Parmadale is a children's village operated by Catholic Charities Health and Human Services. Since its opening in 1925, Parmadale has evolved from a village for children whose parents were deceased or otherwise unable to care for them to meet the needs of the day. Today, Parmadale serves children and families with a history of delinquent behaviors and emotional problems. The children live in cottages in the village and attend Parmadale School, which is operated separately from the residential village.

Parmadale's teens have participated in the traditional summer reading program that encouraged reading for the chance to win drawing prizes. This became rather anticlimactic for the students at the school. I wanted to promote reading and somehow reward all students for their efforts, and I came up with "Reading Is the Ticket." The principal, teachers, and cottage monitors were supportive, and the teens were very excited. Teens from the main classroom, special education, and intensive treatment center were all included.

I arranged for a local hip-hop poet (Q-Nice) to do a program during the last week of the summer school session. Students who completed their summer reading used their entry form as an admission ticket to the program. The program ran for five weeks; the entry form had to be signed by their teacher or cottage monitor to confirm that they had read. Reading one book allowed the teens into the poetry program; reading two books would also make them eligible for some small door prize drawings. The teens filled out the bottom portion of their forms if they wanted to prepare a poem to read aloud at the program.

Q-Nice did some of his performance poetry. In between his poems, teens were called up to read their poetry. He gave the teens honest and positive critiques on their poems and performances; it was evident that this nourished their pride and self-esteem. The program was a huge success. The atmosphere was energetic and respectful, the teens supported each other's performance poetry, and Q-Nice's message to the teens was positive and encouraging. Fifty-seven teens and twenty-six teachers, cottage monitors, and assistants attended. The teens who read their poems were given an autographed poster of Q-Nice. An outside group donated a lunch of pizza, salad, and ice cream following the program because the teens did so well with their summer reading. And the students and staff want to do it again.

Submitted by Bonnie Demarchi, Regional Teen Services Manager, Cuyahoga County Public Library, Parma Regional Library

Summer Reading for Incarcerated Teen Boys

C. A. Dillon Youth Development Center

Butner, North Carolina

I work at a school for incarcerated young men in North Carolina. In the summer of 2005 we had a Readers Choice award competition modeled loosely on the *American Idol* television program and an award program that one of my email clubs has each year. The students nominated twenty-one of their favorite books and voted off one or two books each week until a winner was declared. After six ballots, the winner was *Life in Prison* by Stanley Williams. The school's art department designed a Golden Book Award, and the students wrote letters to Mr. Williams, a death row inmate at San Quentin Prison, asking him to send a representative to the school to receive his award.

Some students resisted participating at first until they realized that the program was fun and nonthreatening. It encouraged students to discuss the books and develop alliances. These shifting alliances caused many books to hold on to the end and some favorites to fall early. Circulation of books increased in general during the program, as well as requests for the books in the competition. I deliberately made the program completely voluntary, with only intrinsic rewards. Whenever a student asked what he was going to get out of it, I simply told him that our reward was that we would let the author know how we feel about his book. The students would ask what kind of reward was that and threw in a profanity or two for good measure, but soon they came around and began to ask about voting if a few days into the week came and went before I gave them the opportunity to do so.

At the time of this submission, the students are writing letters of congratulations and invitation to the author. If he sends someone to receive the award, we will have a culminating award ceremony; if he can't send someone, we will mail the plaque to him.

Submitted by William Prince, C. A. Dillon Youth Development Center

"Read-Iculous" Teen Summer Reading Program 2005 at the Chesterfield Detention Home

Chesterfield County Public Library

Chesterfield, Virginia

The Outreach Services department of the Chesterfield County Public Library has adapted the library's teen summer reading program and implemented it at the Chesterfield Detention Home for several years. As Outreach Services coordinator, I ordinarily handle all services to the incarcerated by our department. Juvenile offenders aged ten through seventeen are housed at the detention home year-round and attend school on the premises. The school is a satellite of the Chesterfield County school system, but it doesn't possess a library on-site. The principal and teachers support the public library's efforts to provide library service, and during the summer the staff work in partnership with us to present an adaptation of the summer reading program.

It has been a challenge serving this population, and prior to the principal's arrival, the detention home staff were lukewarm in welcoming library service to the facility. Juvenile inmates were permitted only minimal contact with outreach staff, who arrived at the facility every Friday with current teen periodicals and book requests that were telephoned into my office by the school's English teacher. Frequently, the magazines were not distributed or not distributed widely. Library books were lost or left the facility with released detainees. Detention home staff were disinterested or unconcerned. Nevertheless, we persevered in our efforts to provide service.

In 2005 I began preparing staff and detainees for the beginning of the Summer Reading Program a week prior to its kickoff in the library branches. I distributed annotated lists of popular YA books to the teens and encouraged them to make personal lists of books they were interested in. Detention home staff prepared a form on which teens could write their requests once a week. I would pick up the form on Monday or Tuesday, pull the books that were requested from the library's collection, and bring them on Friday. I hung posters advertising the summer reading program on the walls. I did a "show-and-tell" of the prizes that would be awarded for the high readers. In 2005 the prizes consisted of coupons for 40 percent off the admission price to Busch Gardens for six people as well as gift certificates for $25 and $15 to the highest and second-highest readers. I did everything to promote the program but a song and a dance, and if I thought I could get away with it, I would have tried it!

Each week for the next six to eight weeks, I showed up at the detention home with books that were requested and magazines. Sometimes it was necessary to leave the materials with the shift coordinator, and I would have to leave with the hope that the materials would be distributed to the teens. Most of the time, I was escorted down to the dormitories where I was allowed to distribute the books and magazines myself. At that time, I passed out reading slips for the teens to write down the titles of books and magazines that they had read in the past week. I welcomed the face-to-face contact with the detainees; they were rarely anything but polite and appreciative. Before leaving, I drew a slip from the ones they had just filled out and gave away a new YA book to the person whose name was on the slip. Each teen was pleased and surprised when I presented him or her with a new book to keep. The following week, I would often receive one or two book slips bearing the title of the awarded book. Not only had the winner read the book, he or she had passed it on to a friend!

When I returned to my office, I wrote each title submitted by the teens onto a personal reading log. At the close of the program, which was in mid-August, when the last title was recorded on the last teen log and the last prize book was given away, I determined the number of registered participants, the number who completed the program by reading the required ten books or magazines, the number of books read, and the top two readers. In 2005 we had sixty-two participants. Seventeen read between 5 and 10 books and four finished the program, and the teens read a total of 251 books and magazines. It is important to remember that the detention home is a short-term facility, and many teens stay only a week or two before they are sent elsewhere. There are never more than fifty-five residents at any given time. Besides, the importance of the program extends beyond the number of participants and number of books that were read. The importance of the program lies in the belief that books and information have the power to change lives. By striving to instill a love of reading in incarcerated teens, maybe we can provide them with an avenue of hope that their lives can be different. Maybe a love of reading will lead them one day to the book that will alter their lives forever.

Submitted by Sherie Parker, Outreach Services Coordinator, Chesterfield County Public Library

Summer Reading for Incarcerated Teens

Austin Public Library

Austin, Texas

In the summer of 2005 Austin Public Library extended its teen summer reading program to Austin's short-term youth detention facility (Gardner-Betts Juvenile Justice Center). At any time, 50–120 kids, aged twelve through seventeen, may be incarcerated at Gardner-Betts. The average stay at the center is nine through twelve days, but some kids stay up to six months. Most of the kids have low levels of reading skills and perform poorly in school. They have gotten in trouble and are in Gardner-Betts awaiting adjudication of their case. We tailored our program to meet the needs of the youth who are incarcerated by adjusting our procedures and including appealing programs.

The summer reading program encourages teens to read four books over the summer. Once they have finished reading four books, they return a form to their local library and receive a prize (in 2005 it was a key chain) and are entered into a grand prize drawing, held at our end-of-summer party, Teen Fest. These procedures don't work with youth who are incarcerated because they are unable to get to a library branch. Instead, we brought the reading program to the center.

A team from the Youth Services division of the library visited the center biweekly to register youths for the 2005 Summer Reading Program—SRP.05. The youths could participate in the reading program solely at the center, or they could also opt to have their book form entered into the library's grand prize drawing. This gave youth who were leaving the center incentive to visit local libraries once they were released. Out of 156 youth, only 19 of them chose to participate solely at the center; the others wanted to be entered into the drawing. In fact, two of the youths from Gardner-Betts won our grand prize drawings—there were ten final prizes. The first winner won tickets for four people to visit theme parks in the area. His mother indicated he had never won anything before, and she almost cried because she was so proud of him. The second youth won a $50 gift certificate to a local department store.

Early on we decided that it was important to provide a reward for reading that strongly matched the purpose of the program—reading for enjoyment. So, instead of the library-wide key chains, the kids at Gardner-Betts received paperback books. Funds from several sources, along with donations from Orca Books and Barnes and Noble, allowed each Gardner-Betts youth who participated to take a brand-new book home upon leaving the center. The teens, who are generally not readers, were very excited about this and spent much care choosing their prize books. Not only did this program ensure that these kids had a book to take with them when they left the center, it was a book they earned, which made it mean much more to them and their families.

The second component of the summer reading program included a biweekly special program that all the youth could participate in. These programs included a writing workshop with author Spike Gillespie, a Capoeira demonstration (Brazilian martial art), and a poetry workshop.

Our first year offering SRP.05 at Gardner-Betts could not have been more successful. A total of 156 youth participated in the reading portion of SRP.05 and a total of 466 teens attended the programs. The cost for books and programs was under $500. The program was designed by Wired for Youth Librarians Patti Cook and Blair Parsons, Library School Intern Amy Wander, and Youth Services Specialist Devo Carpenter under the supervision of Jeanette Larson, Youth Services manager.

Submitted by Jeanette Larson, Youth Services Manager, Austin Public Library

CONTRIBUTORS

Amy Alessio
Teen Coordinator
Schaumburg Township District Library
130 S. Roselle Rd.
Schaumburg, IL 60193
Telephone: (847) 923-3191
Fax: (847) 923-3428
aalessio@stdl.org
http://www.stdl.org

Stacie Barron
Youth Services Librarian
Livingston Parish Library
13986 Florida Blvd.
Livingston, LA 70754
Telephone: (225) 686-2436
Fax: (225) 686-3888
sbarron@pelican.state.lib.la.us
http://www.livingston.lib.la.us

Hope Baugh
Young Adult Services Manager
Carmel Clay Public Library
55 4th Ave., SE
Carmel, IN 46032
Telephone: (317) 814-3979
Fax: (317) 571-4285
hbaugh@carmel.lib.in.us
http://www.carmel.lib.in.us
http://www.reads4teens.org

Linda Brilz
Youth Services Librarian
Boise Public Library
715 S. Capitol Blvd.
Boise, ID 83702
Telephone: (208) 384-4200
Fax: (208) 384-4156
lbrilz@cityofboise.org
http://www.boisepubliclibrary.org

Kate Brown
Teen Services Librarian
Benicia Public Library
150 East L St.
Benicia, CA 94510
Telephone: (707) 746-4741
allison.angell@ci.benicia.ca.us
kbrown@ci.benicia.ca.us
http://www.ci.benicia.ca.us/library.html

Kris Buker
Teen Specialist
Howard County Library, Glenwood Branch
2350 Route 97
Cooksville, MD 21723
Telephone: (410) 313-5583
Fax: (410) 313-5575
bukerk@hclibrary.org
http://www.hclibrary.org

Randee Bybee
Library Assistant, Children's Services
Upland Public Library
450 N. Euclid Ave.
Upland, CA 91786
Telephone: (909) 931-4213
Fax: (909) 931-4209
rbybee@ci.upland.ca.us
http://www.uplandpl.lib.ca.us

Gary Cassel
Webmaster, Flamingnet Book Reviews
8415 Bellona La., Suite 104
Baltimore, MD 21204
Telephone: (410) 215-9020
Fax: (410) 321-0124
gcassel@comcast.net
http://www.flamingnet.com

Karen Cruze
Youth Services Librarian, Teen Specialist
Northbrook Public Library
1201 Cedar La.
Northbrook, IL 60062
Telephone: (847) 272-6224
kcruze@nsls.info
http://www.northbrook.info

Emily Daly
Young Adult Specialist
Natrona County Public Library
307 E. Second St.
Casper, WY 82609
Telephone: (307) 237-4935, ext. 101
Fax: (307) 266-3734
edaly@will.state.wy.us
http://www.natronacountylibrary.org

Karen J. DeAngelo
Youth Services Librarian
Town of Ballston Community Library
2 Lawmar La.
Burnt Hills, NY 12027
Telephone: (518) 399-8174
kdeangelo@sals.edu
http://burnthills.sals.edu

Bonnie Demarchi
Regional Teen Services Manager
Cuyahoga County Public Library
Parma Regional Library
7335 Ridge Rd.
Parma, OH 44129
Telephone: (440) 885-5362
bdemarchi@cuyahoga.lib.oh.us
http://www.cuyahogalibrary.org/branchespages/
    PAR.htm

Geri Diorio
Teen Services Librarian
The Ridgefield Library
472 Main St.
Ridgefield, CT 06877
Telephone: (203) 438-2282
gdiorio@biblio.org
http://www.ridgefieldlibrary.org

Denise DiPaolo
Young Adult Librarian
Rogers Memorial Library
91 Coopers Farm Rd.
Southampton, NY 11968
Telephone: (631) 283-0774, ext. 548
ddipaolo@suffolk.lib.ny.us
http://www.myrml.org

Eileen Dyer
Young Adult Services Librarian
South Kingstown Public Library
1057 Kingstown Rd.
Peace Dale, RI 02879
Telephone: (401) 789-1555, ext. 118
Fax: (401) 782-6370
eileendr@lori.state.ri.us
http://www.skpl.org

Tami Edminster
Program and Product Development Specialist
Indianapolis–Marion County Public Library
2450 N. Meridian St.
Indianapolis, IN 46206
Telephone: (317) 275-4083
Fax: (317) 269-1768
tedminster@imcpl.org
http://www.imcpl.org

Shari Fesko
Youth Teen Services Librarian
Southfield Public Library
26300 Evergreen Rd.
Southfield, MI 48076
Telephone: (248) 796-4331
sfesko@sfldlib.org
http://www.sfldlib.org

Jennifer Garner
Assistant Director/Teen Librarian
North Liberty Community Library
520 W. Cherry St.
North Liberty, IA 52317
Telephone: (319) 626-5701
Fax: (319) 626-5733
jgarner@north-liberty.lib.ia.us
http://www.northlibertylibrary.org

Mari Hardacre
Manager, Young Adults' Services
Allen County Public Library
200 E. Berry St.
P.O. Box 2270
Fort Wayne, IN 46801
Telephone: (260) 421-1200, ext. 1255
mhardacre@acpl.info
http://www.acpl.info/yas/

Dymphna Harrigan
Teen Librarian
Danbury Library
170 Main St.
Danbury, CT 06810
Telephone: (203) 797-4528
Fax: (203) 796-1688
dharrigan@danburylibrary.org
http://www.danburylibrary.org/teenzone/

Melissa Hartson
Young Adult Reference Librarian
Newport Beach Public Library
1000 Avocado Ave.
Newport Beach, CA 92660
Telephone: (949) 717-3808
Fax: (949) 640-5681
mhartson@city.newport-beach.ca.us
http://www.newportbeachlibrary.org

Jean Jansen
Assistant Head of Youth Services
Villa Park Public Library
305 S. Ardmore Ave.
Villa Park, IL 60181
Telephone: (630) 834-1176
Fax: (630) 834-0489
jjansen@linc.lib.il.us
http://www.villapark.lib.il.us

Danielle King
Teen Program Specialist
Orange County Library System
101 E. Central Blvd.
Orlando, FL 32801
Telephone: (407) 835-7323, ext. 6301
king.danielle@ocls.info
http://www.ocls.info

Kevin King
Lead Librarian—Teen Services
Kalamazoo Public Library
315 S. Rose St.
Kalamazoo, MI 49007
Telephone: (269) 342-9837
Fax: (269) 345-6995
kevink@kpl.gov
http://www.kpl.gov

Kristin Lade
Youth Services Librarian
West Bend Community Memorial Library
630 Poplar St.
West Bend, WI 53095
Telephone: (262) 335-5151, ext. 128
Fax: (262) 335-5150
klade@hnet.net, yalibrarianwi@yahoo.com
http://www.hnet.net/~wbcml/

Jeanette Larson
Youth Services Manager
Austin Public Library
800 Guadalupe St.
Austin, TX 78701
P.O. Box 2287
Austin, TX 78768-2287
Telephone: (512) 974-7405
larsonlibrary@yahoo.com
http://www.ci.austin.tx.us/library/

Maria Levetzow
Young Adult Librarian
Bettendorf Public Library
2950 Learning Campus Dr.
Bettendorf, IA 52722
Telephone: (563) 344-8916
Fax: (563) 344-4185
mlevetzow@bettendorf.org
http://www.bettendorflibrary.com/teen/index.htm

Susan Levine
Librarian I
Montgomery County Public Libraries
Silver Spring Library
8901 Colesville Rd.
Silver Spring, MD 20910
Telephone: (301) 565-7689
Fax: (301) 565-7301
susan.levine@montgomerycountymd.gov
http://www.montgomerycountymd.gov/library/

Cathy Lichtman
Teen Services Librarian
Plymouth District Library
223 S. Main St.
Plymouth, MI 48170
Telephone: (734) 453-0750, ext. 230
Fax: (734) 453-0733
clichtman@plymouthlibrary.org
http://plymouthlibrary.org

Mary Maggio
Librarian
Mastics-Moriches-Shirley Community Library
407 William Floyd Pkwy.
Shirley, NY 11967
Telephone: (631) 399-1511
Fax: (631) 281-4442
mmaggio@suffolk.lib.ny.us
http://www.communitylibrary.org

Leslie McCombs
Teen Center Advisor
Ada Community Library
10664 W. Victory Rd.
Boise, ID 83709
Telephone: (208) 362-0181, ext. 2
Fax: (208) 362-0303
lmccombs@adalib.org
http://www.adalib.org

Stephanie McElrath
Youth Services Clerk
Saugerties Public Library
91 Washington Ave.
Saugerties, NY 12477
Telephone: (845) 246-4317, ext. 104
Youth-services@hvc.rr.com
http://saugertiespubliclibrary.org

Ian McKinney
Assistant Manager, Young Adults' Services
Allen County Public Library
200 E. Berry St.
P.O. Box 2270
Fort Wayne, IN 46801
Telephone: (260) 421-1200, ext. 1255
imckinney@acpl.info
http://www.acpl.info/yas/

Mary McKinney
Senior Librarian, Tucson-Pima Public Library
Wilmot Branch Library
530 N. Wilmot Rd.
Tucson, AZ 85711
Telephone: (520) 791-4627
mary.mckinney@tucsonaz.gov
http://www.tppl.org

Martha Mikkleson
Librarian, Young Adult Services
Patchogue-Medford Library
54-60 E. Main St.
Patchogue, NY 11772
Telephone: (631) 654-4700, ext. 257
Fax: (631) 289-3999
mmikkle@suffolk.lib.ny.us
http://pml.suffolk.lib.ny.us

LaDonne Moosman
Youth Services Librarian
Sinte Gleska University Library
P.O. Box 107
105 E. 2nd St.
Mission, SD 57555
Telephone: (605) 856-8100, ext. 8370
ladonne.moosman@sinte.edu

Laura Panter
Adult and Young Adult Librarian
Middle Country Public Library
101 Eastwood Blvd.
Centereach, NY 11720
Telephone: (631) 585-9393, ext. 227
panterlaura@mcpl.lib.ny.us
http://www.mcpl.lib.ny.us

Kimberly Paone
Supervisor, Adult/Teen Services
Elizabeth Public Library
11 S. Broad St.
Elizabeth, NJ 07202
Telephone: (908) 354-6060, ext. 7237/7235
Fax: (908) 354-5845
kpaone@elizpl.org
http://www.njpublib.org

Sherie Parker
Outreach Services Coordinator
Chesterfield County Public Library
9501 Lori Rd.
P.O. Box 297
Chesterfield, VA 23832-0297
Telephone: (804) 748-1768
Fax: (804) 751-4679
parkers@chesterfield.gov
http://library.co.chesterfield.va.us

Shilo Perlman
Teen Coordinator
Boca Raton Public Library
200 N.W. Boca Raton Blvd.
Boca Raton, FL 33432
Telephone: (561) 367-7022
sperlman@bocalibrary.org
http://www.bocalibrary.org

Tracey Pinto
Youth Services Librarian
New Port Richey Public Library
5939 Main St.
New Port Richey, FL 34652
Telephone: (727) 841-4547, ext. 289
Fax: (727) 841-4559
tpinto@nprlibrary.org
http://www.tblc.org/newport/

William Prince
C. A. Dillon Youth Development Center
100 Dillon Dr.
Butner, NC 27509
Telephone: (919) 575-3166, ext. 214
william@princew.com
http://www.ncdjjdp.org/facilities/dillon.html

Melissa S. Rauseo
Young Adult Librarian
Peabody Institute Library
82 Main St.
Peabody, MA 01960
Telephone: (978) 531-0100, ext. 14
Fax: (978) 532-1797
rauseo@noblenet.org
http://www.peabodylibrary.org/ya/yahome.html

Cindy Rider
School Liaison Program Librarian
Vigo County Public Library
One Library Sq.
Terre Haute, IN 47807
Telephone: (812) 232-1113, ext. 294
Fax: (812) 232-3208
crider@vigo.lib.in.us
http://www.vigo.lib.in.us

Bianca Roberts
Manager, Youth Services
St. Louis County Library
1640 S. Lindbergh Blvd.
St. Louis, MO 63131
Telephone: (314) 994-3300
Fax: (314) 997-7602
broberts@slcl.org
http://www.slcl.org

Mary Robinson
Young Adult Services Librarian
Herrick District Library
300 S. River Ave.
Holland, MI 49423
Telephone: (616) 355-3100, ext. 3708
holmr@llcoop.org
http://www.herrickdl.org

Diane M. Sanabria
Young Adult Services Coordinator
Robert Cormier Center for Young Adults
Leominster Public Library
30 West St.
Leominster, MA 01453
Telephone: (978) 534-7522
Fax: (978) 840-3357
dsanabri@leominsterlibrary.org
http://www.leominsterlibrary.org

Betty Sheridan
Young Adult Librarian
Upper Arlington Public Library
2800 Tremont Rd.
Upper Arlington, OH 43221
Telephone: (614) 486-9621
Fax: (614) 487-2044
bsheridan@ualibrary.org, easheridan@yahoo.com
http://www.ualibrary.org

Karen M. Smith
Young Adult Librarian
Allen Park Public Library
8100 Allen Rd.
Allen Park, MI 48101
Telephone: (313) 381-2425
kmsmith@tln.lib.mi.us
http://www.allen-park.lib.mi.us

Sherrill L. Smith
Assistant to the Director
Public Libraries of Saginaw
505 Janes Ave.
Saginaw, MI 48607
Telephone: (989) 755-9822
Fax: (989) 755-2828
s.smith@saginawlibrary.org
http://www.saginawlibrary.org

Denise Stutzman
Librarian I
San Diego County Library
La Mesa Branch
8055 University Ave.
La Mesa, CA 91941
Telephone: (619) 469-2151
denise.stutzman@sdcounty.ca.gov
http://www.sdcl.org

Heather Ujhaz
Assistant Youth Services Coordinator
Akron-Summit County Public Library
60 S. High St.
Akron, OH 44326
Telephone: (330) 643-9186
Fax: (330) 543-9014
hujhazy@akronlibrary.org
http://www.ascpl.lib.oh.us

Lisel Ulaszek
Youth Services Librarian
Gail Borden Public Library
270 N. Grove Ave.
Elgin, IL 60120
Telephone: (847) 608-5011
Fax: (847) 742-0485
lulaszek@nsls.info
http://www.gailborden.info

Margie Walker
YA/Reference Librarian
Amesbury Public Library
149 Main St.
Amesbury, MA 01913
Telephone: (978) 388-8148
Fax: (978) 388-2662
margiewalker@mvlc.org
http://www.amesburylibrary.org

Edna Weeks
Young Adult Services Coordinator, Hawaii State
    Library, Oahu
Hawaii State Public Library System
478 S. King St.
Honolulu, HI 96813
Telephone: (808) 586-3490
Fax: (808) 586-3584
edna@librarieshawaii.org
http://www.librarieshawaii.org

DeAnza Williams
Young Adult Librarian—Hermitage Branch
Nashville Public Library
3700 James Kay La.
Hermitage, TN 37076
Telephone: (615) 880-3951
Fax: (615) 880-3955
deanza.williams@nashville.gov
http://www.library.nashville.org

K. C. Williams
System Director
Sevier County Public Library System
321 Court Ave.
Sevierville, TN 37862
Telephone: (865) 428-7653
Fax: (865) 908-6108
kcwm@sevierlibrary.org
http://www.sevierlibrary.org

Carolyn Witt
Director
Washington Public Library
415 Jefferson
Washington, MO 63090
Telephone: (636) 390-1070
Fax: (636) 390-0171
cwitt@ci.washington.mo.us
http://www.ci.washington.mo.us/Library/Library.htm

Kelley Worman
Young Adult Services Coordinator
Fresno County Public Library
2420 Mariposa St.
Fresno, CA 97320
Telephone: (559) 488-3205
Fax: (559) 488-1971
kelley.worman@fresnolibrary.org
http://www.fresnolibrary.org/teen/

Gigi Yang
Manager of Young Adult Services
Mamie Doud Eisenhower Public Library
3 Community Park Rd.
Broomfield, CO 80020
Telephone: (720) 887-2366
Fax: (720) 887-1384
gyang@ci.broomfield.co.us
http://www.ci.broomfield.co.us/library/

INDEX

Titles of summer reading programs are shown in quotation marks.

Katharine Kan is a freelance library consultant and writer. She conducts workshops on young adult services and on graphic novels in libraries across the country. She reviews graphic novels for *Voice of Youth Advocates* in her column, "Graphically Speaking," and for Diamond Comics Distributors' Bookshelf website for librarians and teachers. She has served on YALSA's Best Books for Young Adults Committee and on the Printz Award Committee, and she chaired the Graphic Novel Task Force from 2003 to 2005. Prior to her consulting activities, Kan worked in the Hawaii State Public Library System for fourteen years, first as a branch young adult librarian and then as head of young adult services at the Hawaii State Library in Honolulu and Oahu-Wide coordinator of young adult services. She then worked for five years as a young adult librarian at Allen County Public Library. Kan earned her MLS from the University of Hawaii at Manoa.